ON POINT

You're On Point!

Tom Brokaw

ENDORSEMENTS

Pam Borton says that "influential positions are not about power or us as the leaders—it's the people that matter." No matter what kind of organization you are leading, if you follow her game plan for ON POINT leadership, everyone wins.

HARVEY MACKAY

New York Times #1 Best-Selling Author of
"Swim With the Sharks Without Being Eaten Alive"

Pam Borton's story is a remarkable one. Leadership, regardless of the arena, is entirely about the art of engaging individuals and their skills and passions in service of a mission that matters. Pam has fiercely demonstrated the desire, drive, and resilience necessary to accomplish meaningful things within her family, community, and teams. In ON POINT, you get a thoroughly enjoyable view into her life and work and an invaluable resource to take you to the next level.

SHARI L. BALLARD

President – U.S. Retail and
Chief Human Resources Officer
Best Buy
Forbes 50 Most Powerful Women in Business (2010, 2011, 2015)

ON POINT is a wonderful journey for any leader in a fast-paced, change-laden environ-ment where every decision and act comes with its own sense of urgency. Pam Borton graces us with a lesson-rich look into the leadership conundrum of college athletics, education, and business. If you're committed to making a difference for the people in your life, and con-sider yourself a life-long learner and educator, then ON POINT won't only enrich you, it will inspire you. Thanks, Pam, for sharing with us and leaving your legacy for the thousands of us you have coached along the way!

SANDY BARBOUR
Athletic Director
Penn State University
Forbes Top 25 Most Powerful People in Sports (2015)

If you are a coach, or think you want to be one, get up off the bench and get ON POINT. Pam Borton's leadership game plan delivers victories above and beyond the scoreboard. I learned a lot from watching Pam's teams. As a leader of people and a true coach, she has few equals on or off the court. I respected Pam as a person and coach and always was impressed with how she motivated her players. Pam recruited the two most recent All-Americans to the Minnesota program, which is a tough place to secure top recruits. I am honored to count her as a friend and colleague.

TUBBY SMITH
Head Coach
University of Memphis Men's Basketball
2016 John R. Wooden Legends of Coaching Award and 1 NCAA Championship

There's a lot more to coaching excellence than winning games. ON POINT reminds coaches to never forget that they are leaders who represent their families, communities, teams, and organizations. Coach Borton knows what it takes to achieve excellence and she brings those lessons off the court and into business and life. Her "people matter" philosophy captures what great coaches understand: that numbers aren't nearly as important as the people attached to those numbers.

GENO AURIEMMA
Head Coach
University of Connecticut Women's Basketball
2011 John R. Wooden Legends of Coaching Award and 11 NCAA Championships

Our family's Carlson Credo guides our collective actions in life and business:
Whatever you do, do with Integrity.
Wherever you go, go as a Leader.
Whomever you serve, serve with Caring.
Whenever you dream, dream with your All.
And never, ever give up.
Pam Borton lives it, every day! She understands the critical elements of leadership: high integrity with yourself and others, life-long learning because every day is an opportunity to improve, and people first because leadership is all about inspiring others. Think like an athlete and always seek coaching no matter what level you achieve—everyone needs a coach! Thank you for sharing this story, the successes and failures, and your learnings along the way. This book will inspire people to take action and be ON POINT.

WENDY CARLSON NELSON
Board of Directors
Carlson Holdings

In ON POINT, Pam Borton shares the ethics, values, and leadership skills honed growing up on a Midwest farm, playing competitive sports, and coaching for 27 years in the pressure cooker of big-time athletics. From the Final Four to the business world, she implements her leadership game plan to lift executive leaders and teams to the next level in work and in life. In Pam's must-read book, you will learn that the process before the contest determines the outcome of the game, and you will receive valuable tools to keep you and your team inspired and on track, and to navigate the high-performance terrain of adversity with grace. Enjoy!

MARK W. SHEFFERT
President and CEO
Manchester Companies, Inc.

The important and compelling lessons on leadership detailed in ON POINT are powerful and moving. This well-written book detailing the life of a high-profile executive is a must-read for aspiring leaders. Brava, Pam!

CHERYL REEVE
Head Coach
Minnesota Lynx (WNBA)

When I think of Pam Borton, I think of a leader who has had an impact on so many people during her years as a collegiate basketball coach. The greatest impact Pam had on me as a player was that she was someone I knew was always there for me. There were plenty of ups and downs during my two years playing for Pam, but no matter what happened on or off the court, I knew that she had her players' best interests in mind. I know that at any time, day or night, I can reach out to her and she will be there for me.

LINDSAY WHALEN
Professional Basketball Player and Olympic Gold Medalist
Minnesota Lynx (WNBA)

Let Pam Borton's wisdom and expertise awaken the ON POINT leader in you! Part memoir, part leadership guide, ON POINT provides practical game plans for leaders in every industry. Pam bares her soul, pours her heart out, and shares her mind and unique life experiences to show us that true coaching is really about developing others, building teams, and celebrating their successes.

AIMEE COHEN
Keynote Speaker, Executive Coach, and Best-Selling Author of
"WOMAN UP! Overcome the 7 Deadly Sins That Sabotage Your Success"

I have been blessed to know Pam Borton for 14 years. I admire her because she has stayed the course, never getting too high or too low, believing in herself, and never compromising from the principles so important to her. Pam sees the big picture, understanding that with challenges come opportunities. Life is about relationships and I am thankful for Pam's leadership, passion, grace, and friendship. She impacted many during her career as a coach and continues to do so today in her work as an executive, consultant, motivational speaker, and now as an author. She is truly ON POINT.

JOEL MATURI
Athletics Director (Retired)
University of Minnesota

It has been my pleasure to know Pam Borton first as the highly successful head coach of the University of Minnesota women's basketball team and later as a good friend. Pam's passion for teaching young adults the skills needed to reach their full potential is boundless. Pam wasn't just coaching young athletes to excel in their sport, she was grooming our next generation of leaders. Pam's knowledge and insight are treasures to be shared.

CHARLES E. SPEVACEK
Senior Partner
Meagher & Geer PLLP

Leaders all need a thought partner, a trusted individual to help us continue to grow. Pam Borton has been that individual for me. She helped me see that people will remember you and continue to respect you for taking the time to develop, empower, and push them to get better.

DIANE "DEE" YOHN
Chief Operating Officer
North Star Resource Group

As the parents of a daughter who played her entire collegiate career under Coach Borton at the University of Minnesota, we rode the Division I roller coaster from start to finish. It was a special and memorable ride led by Coach Borton's approachability, care, discipline, sense of humor, and high expectations. If life lessons such as perseverance, going the distance, loyalty, and making an impact beyond basketball are important to you, then we hope you have an opportunity to spend time with Coach Borton. She has much to offer and always did right by our daughter on and off the court. For that we are grateful.

BOB & JILL FOX
Parents of Emily Fox
University of Minnesota

There are many aspects of Pam's life and journey that I admire, respect, and appreciate. We all know her significant success in leading the Minnesota women's basketball team to a Final Four and seven NCAA berths. For me, it wasn't "what" she accomplished but "how" that I admire most. Pam never wavered from her core values and principles, even when she knew it might cost her a win, fans, parents, or players. Her ethics, integrity, humility, and love of coaching are what I always admired most and still do today. Her transition from coaching young women to becoming an ON POINT executive coach is truly inspiring.

SARAH BUXTON
Former Senior Executive Vice President
Federated Insurance

Pam Borton has proven herself to be an effective leader both on and off the court. Her ability to strategically guide others and coach them to success is evident in both her team and professional record. In her community and professional life, Pam has inspired and coached people and teams to tap into their natural abilities and drive towards success. With her ability to identify both individual and team strengths, Pam builds a foundation of confidence and character that allows those that she leads to identify and achieve their goals. There is no doubt that Pam understands the competitive environment that women face today both in and outside of the workplace. In the game of life, Pam Borton's insight in ON POINT is invaluable in teaching us to play to win.

NANCY E. ANDERSON
Senior Wealth Director
BNY Mellon Wealth Management

I have had the privilege of working closely with Pam Borton since 2011, and my admiration for her energy, drive, focus, and determination is off the charts! The coach in her is an expert at bringing people together, motivating, pressing as needed, and leading both individuals and teams to their goals. The executive in her "gets it" . . . and gets it done. There's always a little fun in her game, but make no mistake—Pam Borton is all about results. She'll make it happen.

JAN BALLMAN
President & CEO
Paradigm Reporting & Captioning

My purpose in working with Pam Borton came down to transition. I watched from afar a strong leader who successfully navigated a difficult and very public transition. During that time, she remained strong and positive then reinvented herself. I believe all of us are in transition, and as I work to transition both my current business and lay the groundwork for the next chapter, Pam's experience helps guide my decision-making. Pam took the time and invested in my vision and helps me to be more accountable to myself. She finds ways to challenge me and develop new ways to lead people. Her strong coaching experience is helping me strengthen our team. Pam provides frank and neutral advice that is not always easy to find in the workplace. With Pam's coaching, I am learning to make substantive changes in my approach to leadership. It is obvious to me that Pam was born to be a coach. With her, I know anything is possible.

LORI SEVIOLA
Chief Executive Officer
PsyBar LLC

As I reflect on my time as a student-athlete and assistant coach under Pam Borton at the University of Minnesota, I can't help but think that she was meant to write this book. In both of these positions, she taught me the key fundamentals that developed me as a confident woman, leader, and coach. If you have the desire to succeed as the leader of your team, ON POINT will get you on the way to achieving your personal and professional goals and serve as an invaluable resource for years to come.

KELLY J. ROYSLAND
Head Coach, Macalester College Women's Basketball
Former Player and Assistant Coach, University of Minnesota

ON POINT

A Coach's Game Plan for Life, Leadership, and Performing with Grace Under Fire

PAM BORTON

New York

ON POINT

Published in New York, New York, by Morgan James Publishing. Morgan James and The Entrepreneurial Publisher are trademarks of Morgan James, LLC. www.MorganJamesPublishing.com

The Morgan James Speakers Group can bring authors to your live event. For more information or to book an event visit The Morgan James Speakers Group at www.TheMorganJamesSpeakersGroup.com.

A **free** eBook edition is available with the purchase of this print book.

CLEARLY PRINT YOUR NAME ABOVE IN UPPER CASE

Instructions to claim your free eBook edition:
1. Download the Shelfie app for Android or iOS
2. Write your name in **UPPER CASE** above
3. Use the Shelfie app to submit a photo
4. Download your eBook to any device

ISBN 978-1-68350-020-9 paperback
ISBN 978-1-68350-021-6 casebound
ISBN 978-1-68350-022-3 eBook
Library of Congress Control Number:
2015911556

Cover Design by:
Chris Treccani
chris@3dogcreative.net

Cover Photo by:
Jody Russel Photography.
jodyrussellphotography.com

Interior Design by:
Megan Whitney
megan@creativeninjadesigns.com

In an effort to support local communities, raise awareness and funds, Morgan James Publishing donates a percentage of all book sales for the life of each book to Habitat for Humanity Peninsula and Greater Williamsburg.

Get involved today! Visit
www.MorganJamesBuilds.com

TO MY PARENTS

For my wonderful upbringing on the farm,
for instilling my values, and
for their unconditional love

AND TO MY LIFELONG PARTNER

My rock, my hero, my love

TABLE OF CONTENTS

Foreword   *1*

Introduction   *5*

PART 1—MASTER THE FRONT COURT   15

Chapter 1: Grace Under Fire   **17**

A Perfect Storm   17

The Resilient Leader   21

Leading With Grace   22

ON POINT Game Plan: Have Grace Under Fire   25

Chapter 2: Leading With Passion   **27**

Finding Passion and Purpose   27

Knowing Your Why   29

Giving Your Heart   30

ON POINT Game Plan: Lead With Passion   31

Chapter 3: Being True to You   **33**

Authenticity   34

Courage, Doubt, and Grit   36

ON POINT Game Plan: Be True to You   39

Chapter 4: Winning Is Never Good Enough   **41**

The Curse of Expectations   42

Defining Victory   43

ON POINT Game Plan: Define Winning   46

Chapter 5: The Experts   **47**

Turning the Other Cheek   47

Keeping Your Chin Up   50

ON POINT Game Plan: Survive the Experts   54

Chapter 6: Fired   **55**

The Last Stand   56

The Final Season   58

The Decision   63

The Comeback   65

ON POINT Game Plan: Survive Your Firing   66

PART 2—BUILD YOUR BENCH   67

Chapter 7: Recruiting, Motivating, and Retaining   **69**

Acquiring the Right People   69

Motivating Each Individual   70

Retaining Top Talent   71

Re-recruiting Talent   74

Avoiding "Yes" People   79

ON POINT Game Plan: Recruit, Motivate, and Retain   80

Chapter 8: Building High-Performing Teams   **81**

From Many to One   82

We Got You, Coach   85

ON POINT Game Plan: Build High-Performing Teams   88

Chapter 9: Creating Champions   89

    Championship Culture   89

    Championship Behavior   91

    Next-Level Performance   94

    ON POINT Game Plan: Create Champions   96

Chapter 10: A Driven and Caring Leader   97

    The Gift of Feedback   98

    The Value of Optimism   100

    The Leader's Identity   102

    ON POINT Game Plan: Be a Driven and Caring Leader   104

PART 3—DOMINATE THE CENTER COURT   105

Chapter 11: Accepting Accountability   107

    Shouldering the Weight   108

    Taking the Heat   110

    ON POINT Game Plan: Accept Accountability   111

Chapter 12: The Loss of Power   113

    Positional Identity   114

    True Power   115

    Power in Transition   117

    ON POINT Game Plan: Own Your Power   120

Chapter 13: Taking Risks   121

    Risk's Rewards   121

    Fear and Comfort   124

    ON POINT Game Plan: Take Risks   126

Chapter 14: Managing Change   **127**

Change or Fail   128

Playbook for Change   130

Change Is a Team Sport   135

ON POINT Game Plan: Manage Change   136

Chapter 15: Building a Business Persona   **137**

Defining "IT"   137

Developing "IT"   139

ON POINT Game Plan: Build Your Business Persona   144

Chapter 16: The X-Factor: Emotional Intelligence   **145**

The New Intelligence   145

Self-Awareness   146

Self-Management   147

Social Awareness   148

Relationship Management   149

ON POINT Game Plan: Lead with Emotional Intelligence   151

Chapter 17: Learning From Failed Leaders   **153**

Learning Life Lessons   153

Learning to Engage   155

Fueled by Failure   156

ON POINT Game Plan: Learn from Failure   159

PART 4—LEVERAGE THE LOCKER ROOM   161

Chapter 18: Securing Team Buy-In   **163**

Achieving Alignment   163

Cultivating Team Dynamics   167

ON POINT Game Plan: Secure Team Buy-In   170

Chapter 19: The Power of Positivity   **171**

Start With Belief   171

Recognize Value and Contribution   173

ON POINT Game Plan: Lead with Positivity   174

Chapter 20: Leading a Multigenerational Workplace   **175**

The Leader as Coach   176

Modern-Day Leadership   177

The Multigenerational Workplace   181

ON POINT Game Plan: Lead Across Generations   183

Chapter 21: Producing Strong Daughters   **185**

Helicopter Parents   186

Back to Basics   188

Mentors for Life   190

ON POINT Game Plan: Produce Strong Daughters   192

Chapter 22: Advice to My Younger Self   **193**

Make It Better   193

People Matter   196

Passion and Belief   198

ON POINT Game Plan: Advise Your Younger Self   199

PART 5—DEFEND THE BACKCOURT   201

Chapter 23: Living With Class   **203**

Clueless and Classless   203

In Search of Class   205

Class Produces Luck   206

ON POINT Game Plan: Live with Class   208

Chapter 24: Winning in Life   **209**

Just Win, Baby   210

Beyond the Scoreboard   211

ON POINT Game Plan: Win in Life   214

Chapter 25: Finding Your Home   **215**

Identify Your Gifts   216

Position for Opportunity   217

Broaden Your Horizons   219

Take Flight   220

ON POINT Game Plan: Find Your Home   221

Chapter 26: A True Coach Is Rare   **223**

ON POINT Game Plan: Be a True Coach   227

Chapter 27: Enjoy the Journey   **229**

ON POINT Game Plan: Enjoy the Journey   234

About the Author   *235*

Acknowledgments   *237*

Are You ON POINT?   *243*

FOREWORD

I n May 2003, my life partner Pam was offered the head women's basketball coaching position at the University of Minnesota. We were both so excited about this opportunity and had heard many great things about the school and the city of Minneapolis.

As she flew out for her press conference, our excitement about the future—our future—grew. Within hours of the end of the press conference, I began to wonder what we had signed up for. I'd like to say when Pam was announced as the Minnesota head coach that the media gave her a fair review, but they were so caught up in ridiculing the athletics administration for hiring an "unknown" that they never gave her a chance. They complained that she had little experience and they openly doubted if she could lead a Big Ten team that had just gone to the NCAA Tournament. The media didn't believe she could possibly have what it would take to lead Minnesota women's basketball to the next level.

They were dead wrong. Through hard work and excellent leadership, Pam led the program to its first and only Final Four. Still, the start to her Minnesota career was telling about the environment we were entering. I can now say, many years later, the environment helped shape her—it made her resilient, taught her important lessons, and molded her into the exceptional leader she is today.

The next 12 years would provide an unforgettable experience and, in retrospect, supply a wonderful "training ground" for a leader. Through 12 years, each student-athlete, staff member, team, season, practice, and game required a unique approach and a specific mindset. And, each offered a wonderful new experience. There were many highs, definitely some lows, and all those in-between times, when leadership can really lay the groundwork for the future. Pam learned so much as the head coach at Minnesota—about what it takes to be not just a leader, but to be a great leader. Although we all would love to consider ourselves good leaders, the truth is that leaders are shaped by their environment and their response to it. We all can improve. Pam learned and improved, and I with her—analyzing her successes and mistakes and observing others' successes and mistakes.

As we entered Pam's final season, we both felt the weight and stress attached to the feeling that the year might be her last. It was clear to both of us that even an NCAA Tournament berth and a win or two in the tournament probably wouldn't change the plans of the decision-makers. Yet, as challenging as the last year was for both of us, it also had its rewards. Sometimes knowing your future is decided, no matter what you do, can be almost freeing. Pam embraced her staff and team every day. She relished and enjoyed every moment with them. She would come home late at night, relating wonderful tales of success or stories of another injury or challenge, but always with a smile on her face and with the determination to make the best of the situation.

As I watched her coach that season, it was so obvious what she had become: an unbelievable, inspiring leader. She was coaching her best basketball ever and was enjoying every moment with her team and staff. She was navigating a stressful situation in a hostile environment with a grace and calmness that few could have managed. And, on the day the decision-makers let her go, I thought I could never be prouder of her and how she handled it all. Then, she even proved me wrong.

It's been almost two years since Minnesota let her go. In that short time, Pam has transformed herself. She has taken her passion for and expertise in coaching and teaching, combined with 27 years of experience in major-college athletics, and created two non-profits and a robust executive coaching and consulting business. She built all of it based on her desire to help people be the best they can be. Could I be any prouder now? I wouldn't bet against it. Pam always finds the next level.

This book shares Pam's insights and experiences in growing to become an exceptional leader. We both laughed and cried while she wrote it; if you look carefully, you will find her heart and soul in these pages. I hope you enjoy reading about her journey and that it helps you be the best leader you can be.

Lynn Holleran, *March 2016*

INTRODUCTION

"Books are the quietest and most constant of friends; they are the most accessible and wisest of counselors, and the most patient of teachers."
–Charles W. Eliot–

Through my college coaching career, I always thought it was normal to have darkened, triple bags under my eyes. The exhaustion, stress, bright lights, cameras, recruiting wars, helicopter parents, vicious media, ego-driven AAU and high school coaches, undeniable pressure, unrealistic expectations, and public scrutiny were constants. My job depended on the performance of 18- to 22-year-old kids and our success hung on their mental, physical, and emotional stability on any given day. Regardless, I loved every minute of my journey, I have no regrets, and I would not change one thing. I learned as much from my players as they did from me. Today, I learn as much from my clients as they do from me as their coach.

I grew up in Northwest Ohio on a hog and cattle farm with 100 acres of crops—with three sisters and no brothers. Four girls and no boys on a farm wasn't what my dad had planned. Because of this line-up, I was forced into roles and responsibilities that I accepted without question. I didn't like them but I accepted them and knew it was best for my family, especially my dad. For 36 years during the day, my dad worked in a factory making tires, and for 40 years by night and on weekends, he was a farmer. As he transitioned every day from one job to the other, I watched closely how he was able to get so much done successfully. It was a family routine and best practice to sit down at the dinner table together every evening from 4:00 to 4:30 p.m.

My mother was a stay-home mom and worked harder than anyone I had ever met. To this day, no one works harder than she did. I think she had triple bags under her eyes, too. She was an influencer and leader in our household in many ways. Besides taking care of her own four children, and supporting my dad through his two full-time jobs, she also ran a day care in our home. On most days we had 15 other kids in our house, ranging from infants to middle school age, who would get dropped off from the school bus until their parents picked them up after work. I watched closely how mom nurtured, loved, cared for, disciplined, led, and role modeled for every child she helped raise for over 12 years. She was clear in setting expectations and she negotiated and influenced every child to eat their vegetables—something their own parents couldn't do successfully. It was amazing to watch and I learned so much. I learned more about effective and positive nurturing leadership in my own household growing up from my parents than most people do in a lifetime. I learned more from them than I did from anyone about leadership.

Coaching major-college athletics wasn't a typical 9-to-5, Monday through Friday job. Today, I listen to people in the business world say how hard they work, how tough their jobs are, and how tired they are all the time. I see some people start their days at 10:00 a.m. and end them at 4:00 p.m., considering that a busy and full day for them. More power to you if you can reach your goals and dreams doing this. I never knew any other way than the way my motor runs now and continues to run. It's been in my blood my whole life; I only know one speed and my mind as a strategic and visionary thinker works the same way. For almost three decades, the brutal profession of coaching college athletics was my "job" but it was really my hobby. Fourteen hours a day, seven days a week, 365 days a year, missing most holidays with my family, I loved it and lived it. And, it consumed me.

The pressure mounted as each season went on. The more we won, the greater the expectation was from me as a coach and from the players. The longer I stayed at the same institution, the more *the experts* stifled me with pressure. The average shelf-life for most college coaches, similar to CEOs, is approximately seven years and it could be less in today's environment. The shelf-life of a coach for a professional sports team is at best half of that. The world today and our stakeholders expect instant gratification and winning results, and they want it fast. Gone are the days when stakeholders, boards, and bosses give you sufficient time to build a healthy culture, a solid foundation, and processes to do work the right way. Look around—coaches, presidents, athletic directors, CEOs, project managers, team leaders—if they can't get it done, and soon, they wind up in the hot seat in no time.

The triple bags under my eyes have experienced and seen it all. With a very good friend and mentor, the president of a *Fortune 500* company, I have compared the bags under our eyes every weekend as we shared war stories of our "hobbies" in our very different worlds and industries. What we found was that we shared many of the same challenges.

It seemed like every Big Ten game I coached came down to the last two minutes or last few possessions. We played two to three times a week every season for 12 years. There were many sleepless nights, hours of film, late-night recruiting calls, hours mentoring and nurturing former and current players, and more frequent-flyer miles than I could ever track. When I was home, I wasn't really home or present. The coach's life was consuming in every way imaginable and it integrated into and weaved through my life until it crowded out almost everything else. It is very hard and grueling for a coach's spouse and I would wish that on no one. I would wonder all the time, *Why would anyone ever want to be with a college coach?* It's brutal and harder on your partner or spouse than it is on the coach. So, whenever I turned around and my partner was still there, I counted my blessings and expressed my thanks for her perseverance in putting up with me and the crazy coaching lifestyle.

Strangers would come up to me often and, on occasion of the first time they met me, they would say, You look so much prettier and taller in person than you do on national TV. I would just laugh and with a smile I'd ask, *How am I supposed to take that?* I guess it was the triple bags during the grind of the season that made me appear so intense, intimidating, hyper-focused, and exhausted . . . in a pressure cooker with the world watching me do my job in the spotlight.

On many levels and across industries, companies and high-level leaders combine the lessons, analogies, narratives, and experiences from athletics that comprise lessons about how to take on and to prevail in the face of tough business challenges. Leaders and organizations are afraid that the entire enterprise may come tumbling down because it is too slow to adapt to the urgent, constant change taking place in the environment. Business leaders today are asked to achieve the unthinkable and, many times, with unrealistic expectations attached.

ON POINT combines lessons, narratives, successes, mishaps, and a game plan in each chapter from my experiences in athletics, academics, and business for taking one's leadership and life to the next level with grace. More than ever before in our lifetime, the expectations of leaders are taking on a life of their own. The leader's role in athletics and business is recognized as pivotal to organizational success. With four generations in the workplace, the struggle to recruit and to retain top talent in competitive industries, to understand and embrace the Millennial generation and impacts of social media, to function effectively as a team, to lead in a complicated world when everyone feels they can do it better, and to cope with the mounting expectations and stresses in our society is at an historic level and treads into dangerous territory. In the arms race that is athletics, coaches transform into CEOs, athletic directors transform into business managers and fundraisers, parents turn into their kid's agents, and kids become a generation where they've had everything done for them. How do you lead effectively in the midst of all of this chaos, complexity, and multi-directional change? This is just a taste of the challenges we face in athletics and, similarly, in business.

People and leaders are measured not just on what they achieve, but in the legacy they build through influencing, reaching, and helping people achieve as students, employees, leaders, players, or friends. In everything that we do, it's the people who matter. We all affect people—we either make a positive or negative impact or we have no impact at all. Most of us had someone who has made the biggest impact on our lives and has influenced us as kids or adults, and many would say it was a coach they once had. Most of us can relate these stories from memory with a smile on our faces as if it were yesterday. Competitive athletics provides many examples and is the best arena I know to develop the character, leadership, and resilience needed in today's competitive business world.

It is challenging for executives to effectively communicate an inspiring vision, to align their teams to their organizational strategy, and then to execute it. Many need help and support with their leadership style to learn to lead and to manage people effectively. Being ON POINT does not come naturally for most people; leading teams is not easy and being part of a team is entering unchartered waters for many. There isn't a manual that someone hands you when you join a team, if you get asked to lead a team, or if you slide inches over and sit in the CEO's or head coach's chair. It's easy to say you can do things better and that you would do it differently when you're in that position, but when and if you are ever there, it's like nothing you have ever experienced. You will never be fully prepared until you are in it. A long-time executive coach of 30 years, whom I respect a great deal, recently told me that I had the opportunity to turn executive coaching on its side—leading executive men, women, and teams in business. They noted that no one in the executive coach space blends my background or unique experience leading teams. Having operated at the executive level, I have been there and I have practical experience, I understand and have learned from Millennials, and I'm an expert in coaching and leading teams.

Are you evaluated by wins and losses? Do you live and work in an environment where you feel like you can't afford failure as the end result? We often become a product of the score and the scoreboard places us on the winning team or the losing team in every game. This reflects every game ever played and now represents the conditions of our business lives. Over time, it has become less about the game and more about the peripheral distractions such as the experts and the other circus sideshows. Three decades ago, I wanted to be a coach because

I loved the game, I was an educator at heart, I loved to compete and win, and I considered practice the best time of the day. The job changed overnight. I was now the CEO of my program and it was more about the business side of things than teaching the game itself.

As a former player and a coach, here's what I learned: the process we follow before the contest determines if you win or loss. This book combines lessons and anecdotes, representing real and practical experience, from athletics, business, and my players, bosses, mentors, coaching staff, and clients. It's part memoir and part leadership roadmap. It's my own blood, sweat, and tears. It's about the process I followed in athletics, and that I know works for the clients I coach today.

Deans of business schools, CEOs, athletic directors, presidents at college institutions, head coaches, lawyers, accountants, dads, moms, agents, and Millennials have reached out for advice, coaching, mentoring, and consulting. Each is experiencing dramatic change in the cultures and environments in which they live and work. The way we lead, the people we surround ourselves with, and the understanding that we will never accomplish anything unless we figure out how to positively affect and to bring out the best in others, are the keys to being a successful leader. Until leaders can embrace and learn to lead others effectively and to realize it is not about them, it will be a short stop in that chair. Influential positions are not about power or about us as the leaders—it's the people who matter.

All industries share a similar sense of urgency, instant gratification, technological change, success and failure, and competitive threats. It has become a daunting task and almost impossible to manage the competing priorities and often conflicting needs. We are not working less, but more. The pressure and expectations to win and to drive results to our bottom lines outpace our capabilities . . . and everyone is watching. Developing leaders, enabling high-performing teams, and facilitating succession planning have become top priorities. Every industry faces a generational shift in leadership over the next few years; look around and observe who may be ready to take over or to move up into leadership positions. The answer has been few to none. The talented Millennial generation has arrived and it's our responsibility to embrace them, to coach and develop them, and to enable them to lead. You might learn a lot from them, as I have. If not, get started building relationships and generating collaboration—they will be your bosses very soon.

We all naturally focus on the wins and losses and on how we can be better. Many people are results-driven and focus on the bottom line. By reading ON POINT, I'm assuming you're already an over-achiever or want to be one and become the best at what you do. My goal and expectation in ON POINT is to coach you to focus on the process, to value the importance of people, and to invest in elements that comprise a true leader. Through the game plans provided in this book, you will consistently achieve the results you want, personally and professionally, and make a difference in others' lives as well as your own.

ON POINT focuses more on what happens before and after the wins and losses, rather than during the game. This book will give you the game plan and tools necessary to keep you and your team inspired and on track, and to navigate the high-performance terrain with grace through adversity. When the game starts, you and your teams will be ready to perform and to claim your victory.

Through the chapters that comprise the five key parts in ON POINT, you will learn to develop a culture with your own values, leadership style, and a level of commitment that delivers consistent results—on and off the court or in the board room. Whether it's a family, business, non-profit, or sports team, the strategies shared in this book will help you achieve your desired results while you enjoy the journey. You will transform yourself, your team, and your organization to focus on the process, people, and performance. Considering today's environment and speed of change, a culture of personal and professional leadership development is critical. Those who seek coaching and mentoring are secure and confident in their own skin—and are committed to be the best.

Avoid regret. If you're rushing through life laser-focused on the destination, on how many wins you have, on how many "likes" you have, or on how many friends you have, you're focusing on the wrong things. Shift your focus from quantity to quality. If everyone has a passion and purpose in what they are doing and feel valued, listened to, and more, incredible success will follow.

During a 40-minute game, a basketball team will experience countless challenges and shifts in momentum and must make many critical decisions in seconds, none of which can be reversed, in a quest for victory. Succeeding in this fast-paced, highly competitive environment with thousands and sometimes millions watching requires everyone to perform ON POINT, always at their best. The ON POINT leader accepts and cherishes the responsibility to lead and to make victory possible.

I have cracked the code to inspire individuals and to develop high-performing teams during my 27 years in coaching athletics, and have transferred these skills successfully to the business world as an executive coach. Businesses today no longer have the luxury to develop people slowly and to grow their teams in their spare time. Failure is not an option, and leaders and talents must be identified rapidly and tapped so that no one sits on the sidelines, but leaps to new levels through proper coaching, training, and opportunity. Leveraging real experience in the crucible of leadership, and I provide a practical and proven approach for leaders to learn an effective process to drive peak self-performance and to build high-performing teams.

I'm also passionate about changing the face of leadership, so more women can rise to every level by supporting their needs, mentoring to grow their expertise, and building confidence. We need more women at the top leading people and teams. I want women to survive, navigate, and thrive in the pursuit of leadership, confidently and purposefully. Men are an important part of this process and educating and engaging them are critical. The many men in my life have been some of my most fervent, attentive supporters and have mentored and helped me go to the next level in the business world as a coach. There have been a few women, but not enough. We need more women who pull each other up when we are down, not critiquing and picking each other apart every time we turn around. I'm out to change that mindset, one woman (and man) at a time.

I've done it, successfully. And I continue to learn and to lead in the greatest, most venerable arena: life. Now, let's go and catapult you to the next level by focusing our time ON POINT.

TO THE READER

ON POINT contains five parts, each designed to share crucial, pivotal, and expert plans to support your learning and practical application.
The illustration below depicts the five-part playing court and definitions.

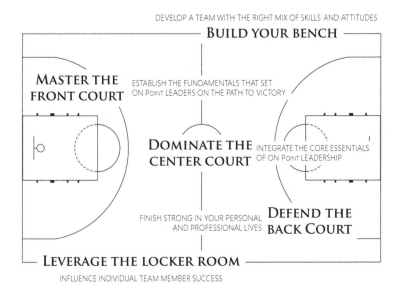

DEVELOP A TEAM WITH THE RIGHT MIX OF SKILLS AND ATTITUDES

BUILD YOUR BENCH

MASTER THE FRONT COURT — ESTABLISH THE FUNDAMENTALS THAT SET ON POINT LEADERS ON THE PATH TO VICTORY

DOMINATE THE CENTER COURT — INTEGRATE THE CORE ESSENTIALS OF ON POINT LEADERSHIP

FINISH STRONG IN YOUR PERSONAL AND PROFESSIONAL LIVES — **DEFEND THE BACK COURT**

LEVERAGE THE LOCKER ROOM

INFLUENCE INDIVIDUAL TEAM MEMBER SUCCESS

PART ONE

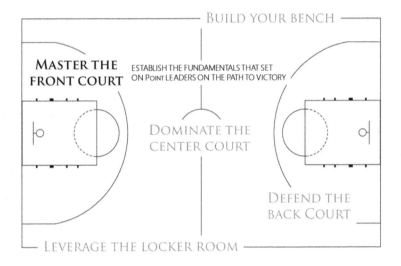

BUILD YOUR BENCH

MASTER THE FRONT COURT ESTABLISH THE FUNDAMENTALS THAT SET ON POINT LEADERS ON THE PATH TO VICTORY

DOMINATE THE CENTER COURT

DEFEND THE BACK COURT

LEVERAGE THE LOCKER ROOM

GRACE UNDER FIRE

"Life is 10 percent what happens to us and
90 percent how we react to it."
—Charles R. Swindoll—

You can't truly know how you will handle adversity, chaos, or extreme situations until you actually stare them in the face. Nothing will ever prepare you for the worst of these situations. Taking a class, listening to a podcast, reading a best-selling book, or attending a seminar—none of these will prepare you adequately. You have to go through the storm to really know what I'm talking about.

A PERFECT STORM

M y 27-year basketball coaching career, and 12-year tenure at the University of Minnesota, gave me valuable, leadership-affirming storms to weather and fires to extinguish. In the 2005-2006 season, a firestorm engulfed me. I learned a key ON POINT lesson: to conduct yourself with grace under fire, you must brave the heat and dance among the flames.

The 2005-2006 Minnesota Gopher women's basketball team wasn't only one of the deepest and most talented—it was also one of the most *unsuccessful*—"teams"

I ever coached. Conditions began to unravel early in the season and it only got worse as the season unfolded. First, the team was spoiled. Two of the world's best players, Gophers in 2004-2005, had graduated or exhausted their eligibility. The returning players, the fans, and the coaching staff were accustomed to putting All-Americans on the floor, and we would have none this season. We were spoiled by talent and the expectations it brought.

The remaining players were not used to taking on roles of higher responsibility, greater consistency, more production, and deeper accountability for keeping the program at a national level. After reaching three consecutive NCAA Tournament Sweet 16s and a Final Four, there was an elite level of expectation. It was now someone else's turn to take on a bigger role, to step up, to be a leader, to be put in pressure situations, and to make plays. My coaches and I had to learn a different way to coach, motivate, and win without All-Americans. We had to learn to grind it out, to rely on many and not just one or two players, and to figure out ways to win without elite star performers. Unfortunately, these conditions created a "you-know-what" storm we were unprepared to manage.

From February on, our team was failing and falling fast—on and off the court. As a head coach, I look back and know that I made mistakes. There was a lack of discipline expected off the court from players and ineffective communication and accountability from my captains and players. I focused too much on what had worked in the past, which seemed natural, but it wasn't working with this team.

This team was unique, like every team is each year. They were struggling and frustrated, and no one in our program was used to losing after three years of 25+ wins and deep runs into the NCAA Tournament. I was focused on the vision and the execution as the leader, but did not have the buy-in from my players, team, and all of my staff. Without buy-in, getting everyone believing and heading in the same direction, we all ended up with different agendas.

Our loss to the University of Washington in the first round of the NCAA Tournament ended the season. After the sudden and unexpected loss, I sat dejectedly and angrily in the press conference in front of dozens of cameras. A reporter asked me a very sensitive question about our star player, whom I had pulled from the game and benched in the second half. She wasn't performing up to the level our team needed and I gave a couple other players in her position those minutes. We were losing and I felt I needed to try something different.

The reporter's question inflamed my passions and the entire year's frustration boiled to the surface. In response to the question, I said too much about this player. I threw her under the bus. I did not think before I spoke because I was angry and I hated to lose. I should have re-directed the question, which is what I usually did. What I should have said was that I needed to evaluate not just this game, but also the last two months of the season. My response was unacceptable from a program of our stature and demonstrated an uncharacteristic lack of leadership. It was a harsh leadership lesson forged in the inferno of competitive disappointment . . . and it was just the beginning.

As I left the press conference, thoughts of what I would change if I had a "do-over" rushed through my mind. But before I could start rebuilding my approach to a successful team, the other shoe dropped. A couple of weeks after the season ended, five players left the program and I fired an assistant coach. This was the perfect storm; the situation gained momentum like a snowball rolling downhill that couldn't be stopped. One at a time, players came to my office and quit the team. Over and over, they walked in and out until five players left within 10 days. It was a nightmare. On top of this, six players—my leaders—were graduating, making a total of 11 players who would not be returning to the program.

The media made me out to be a monster, building a case that there was something wrong with the program. Our firestorm became national news in the women's college basketball world. No one ever knew the real reasons why each player had left the program. Of course I knew, and my administrators and campus leadership knew, the whole story behind each departure, but that was all confidential information. When you are dealing with 18- to 22-year-old young adults who experienced a trying season full of drama, decisions often are made purely on emotion. For some, it was easier to run away from challenging times and issues than to stay and work through them. But, while we may try to run away from our problems, they follow us wherever we go.

I could write a separate book on the 2005-2006 season called "The Perfect Storm" (with title royalties to the best-seller by Sebastian Junger) but I will do my best to summarize the key lessons here. There was much I can't share, but some information is public knowledge. Two of the players left because they were academically ineligible to return to school. Another player exited because she was abused growing up and needed to move closer to family to help her deal with this pain. The fourth player departed to return home after experiencing a significant personal health situation the year before. The fifth player stayed in school but abandoned her playing career because she got caught up in this storm. Today, publicly, I continue to choose to take the high road and to protect each one of the players who left the program.

Ultimately, as a leader, navigating the storm was my responsibility and there were many things I should have, could have, and wish I had done differently. I thought winning would solve and hide all the problems. It didn't—and it made matters worse when we started losing. Entering the NCAA Tournament, I focused on making a run to another Sweet 16 or Final Four, expecting that to erase the season's challenges. Unfortunately, reality intervened and the unproductive conditions swirling around the team resulted in a "one and done" NCAA Tournament.

With much support from my mentors, family, and friends, I took the bullets and daggers that I faced (and read about for a long time) with grace. I refocused my efforts outside of myself to where it should be: on my players. Keeping my job was far down the list. My priority was to protect the players who left the program, for their own personal reasons and challenges, and to support the players who remained. As I accepted the public media and private emotional burden for the departed players, many said I was crazy. But they were just kids and I chose to honor my obligation as a leader to protect them. Like most parents of college kids, I'm sure many of their parents didn't have the full story. They needed support, and I was in the position to provide it.

Fighting through the 2005-2006 "perfect storm" while demonstrating grace under fire was one of the most difficult times I endured as a coach. It paid off in the long run; the experience and lessons steeled me to any future adversity, personally and professionally. Weathering the storm gave me resilience to face the toughest of situations with resolve, belief, confidence, and courage head on. It taught me whom to trust, and I learned how important it is to surround myself with the right people. I became a better coach and a more resilient leader.

THE RESILIENT LEADER

Resiliency is a critical need in leadership in the business world, in athletics, and in our personal lives. Many times in college athletics, a head coach feels like their primary function is to put out fires every day. Leaders in business feel the same way and they wonder: *When is it going to stop? When will I get to my list, when will things go as planned? Will there ever be a time when someone tells me I am on the right path, that I have done a good job?* In our personal lives, a trying marriage, financial challenges, or health issues in our families challenge us to be resilient.

The ON POINT leader must face these challenges and circumstances, building resilience on top of a foundation of confidence and courage. Through the toughest of times, when you are challenged to exercise grace under fire, you are going to need a heavy dose of both on your leadership journey.

Our daily lives are hectic and we often think that the unexpected happens to someone else far, far away. Have you ever considered what might happen if you had to face the unexpected? I experienced numerous "unexpecteds" during my coaching tenure. The most important lesson I learned was to maintain grace while under fire by the media, boosters and donors, fans, and many others, while in a high-profile position. My everyday performance (good or bad) was public knowledge in the media, on television, on the radio, and in every social media outlet. I chose to take the high road, took responsibility, handled the unexpected with grace, and it paid off tenfold.

The first "unexpected" test surfaced immediately upon my May 2002 appointment as head coach at the University of Minnesota. I arrived to lead a program and athletic department under NCAA investigation for many recruiting violations. When I walked through the door, the department was without an athletic director; a week later, the University's president and the chief of staff who hired me departed for the University of Texas.

At the age of 36, my big opportunity looked less than ideal. Yes, I was taking over a Big Ten basketball program, but it was a program with undisclosed NCAA violations, no athletic director, and a president who bolted for another institution. Still, I felt ready and was enthusiastic for the challenge. Maybe I had too much confidence, courage, and resilience, or maybe I was naïve. The task at hand instantly became more difficult than what I had signed up for . . . was I prepared for this? Knowing what I do now, I don't think anyone could prepare him or herself fully for something like this, at any age. I would have to rely on my confidence and courage, and trust that the greater the risk, the greater the reward. And, whatever the outcome, building resiliency would be part of the reward.

From this less-than-auspicious start, resiliency became a hallmark of my career at the University of Minnesota, from beginning to end. In life and work, there will be many times of adversity, trials and tribulations, and fires that leaders face every day and there is only one option that ends well—to learn to have grace when the worst is staring you down. If you choose to blame others, to not take responsibility, and to not take the high road to protect your people and institution, it will ALWAYS come back to haunt you.

LEADING WITH GRACE

The ability to reflect on and to transfer my basketball coaching experience is a key reason my clients hire me as their executive coach. My experience in athletics, similar to those of leaders in business and the community, exposed me to the rhythms of success as well as the searing lessons of failure. Every high-level leader faces daily situations when individuals, teams, and performance break down—when taking the high road and displaying grace while under fire may be the difference between winning and losing.

To be an ON POINT leader, you must surround yourself with thought leaders and support from those who have real experience and who have been in the trenches. Those who have "been there" know the loneliness a leader feels and know, in the long run, that staying the course pays off.

A number of my clients have encountered the unexpected and are learning to leverage their experience with positivity and grace while they continue to put out fires. It is daunting to understand and to accept the responsibility when you agree to sit in that leadership chair. All eyes are on you, and the buck starts and stops with you. Some professionals wilt under the pressure, and some choose not to accept the mantle of leadership in the first place.

It is powerful to face the unexpected, to take action, and to come out on the other side (often not unscathed!). These experiences build and build, layer upon layer, and you become resilient in managing chaos and converting adversity into opportunity. You learn to become a proactive and purposeful leader, better prepared for the next unexpected moment that you will face. As unexpected moments arrive, they will look a bit different each time, but the scars you earn and knowledge you gain will ready you for a new battle.

The 2013-2014 season was my last year coaching at the University of Minnesota, and presented a culminating opportunity for resiliency. The final season placed me in a highly visible and public role, requiring me to demonstrate grace while under fire for over a year. Everyone was watching my every move.

The emotional, mental, and physical toll of the final two seasons was exhausting. As I describe in Chapter 2, leaving a 12-year position and a successful program that I had built was one of the most difficult things I have ever experienced. The program I built made me the winningest coach in program history and, more importantly, had positively influenced the lives of my players and coaches. Despite being fired, I left my office and my program with grace. I had no regrets and walked away with my head held high, with integrity, and with the knowledge I had put everything I had into the program . . . blood, sweat, and tears.

A positive consequence of the unexpected is often the necessity to re-evaluate. Difficult times in our lives cause reflection. We rally those closest to us for support. We consider how much joy we are garnering from our journey and we begin treating others and ourselves as if it's our last day.

In difficult times, the ON POINT leader must take responsibility to stop their people from focusing on what they're not good at and instead start recognizing what they're great at. Truly effective leaders motivate people by recognizing their strengths, focusing on the positives, and getting to people's passions quicker. Move on to the next play, the next account, the next opportunity, and make sure your team is coming with you. While intangible and difficult to encode, a skill in turning away from shortcomings and focusing on strengths is critical for the ON POINT leader.

Perspective teaches us that life is so fragile. Reputations are fragile. Even success is fragile. When we come under fire or disaster strikes, we learn about our own courage. We learn about our ability to triumph over it and to conquer our fears. We learn to be resilient leaders. When the going gets tough, I want you to get public. Be out and about. I want you to be present at the table of your circle of influence. Do not stop what you're doing; charge forward with grace. This is what true leaders do.

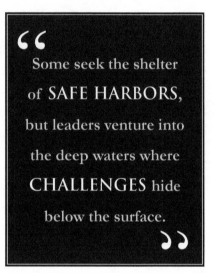

> " Some seek the shelter of **SAFE HARBORS,** but leaders venture into the deep waters where **CHALLENGES** hide below the surface. "

These are the moments in which we learn what we're made of. We find out who is there for us and we discover the strength of the fabric of our relationships. As a leader, the only choice is to learn and to move forward. An effective athletic coach would say, *This play is over; learn from your mistakes and focus on the next play.* Disappointment—and even devastation—is indeed temporary. Handle it with grace and take the high road. This is the essence of ON POINT leadership.

Grace under fire defines a competency you can't be born with; it is a skill you must develop to possess, a consolidation of your life experiences and the resilience you earn through trial by fire. Once gained, it is an intangible, key competency that successful and authentic leaders bring to the table and to critical situations. As you lead with grace, you must control your emotions under the umbrella of extreme adversity that every leader faces. This capability separates the good from the extraordinary leaders.

At different points in our lives, we find ourselves in positions where situations do not end the way we dreamed they would. The script is not how we wrote it. How you handle the fires and the grace you bring will pay off in the long run. For executives, even the intentional ones, adversity and challenges inevitably arise. New executives experience the pressure of developing their unique vision and constructing a team to deliver it. Late-stage executives find it difficult to control their exit and stay the course as they envisioned it for many years. Work, like life, rarely goes as planned.

Let others find safety and live in comfort. I want you, the ON POINT leader, to travel beyond the harbor. Don't be sheltered from dangers, be fearless and face them. Courage and confidence can't unleash their full power in the presence of fear and discomfort.

I have been there, through the storm and in the fire. I have fought public and private battles and earned a great gift: it is a rich life and worth the ride. Now, with time to reflect, I know I am obligated to pass on the gift. If I do not encourage and support others to step up, who will be the next generation of ON POINT leaders to grow and to change our communities and organizations for the better?

ON POINT GAME PLAN: HAVE GRACE UNDER FIRE

+ Take responsibility always; YOU are the leader
+ Do not blame others
+ Think before speaking
+ Take the high road; it will pay off in the long run
+ Protect your team, your people, and the organization
+ Do the right thing and maintain your integrity at all times
+ Embrace adversity; it forges resilience

LEADING WITH PASSION

"They may forget what you said, but they will
never forget how you made them feel."
—Carl W. Buechner—

No matter what industry, profession, or activities embody your work, your ability to lead with passion is critical to success. People have debated for many years about the most important characteristic or "ingredient" for leadership. Hundreds (if not thousands) of books and articles wander the leadership landscape, dissecting corporate, athletic, political, and social leaders' lives in an urgent search for leadership's holy grail.

Theories abound, but a single foundational attribute to leadership success emerges from my experience in business and basketball: PASSION. This is the foundation of an ON POINT leader.

FINDING PASSION AND PURPOSE

Are YOU leading with passion? Do you model passionate leadership and engage people from the heart? Do your team members, colleagues, co-workers, family, and friends know what feeds your passion? Your first focus as a leader should be to identify sources of your inspiration. Then, you can leverage them to enhance the natural talents you have in inspiring others.

Many of us struggle with determining our meaning in life and our deeper WHY. I often get asked the question: *What comes first, my purpose or my passion?* My answer: *It depends.* We can answer this question on an individual basis. It's a combination of discovering why we do what we do and examining our stage in life. Here's what I've found.

A younger person will lead with passion and, ultimately, their emotional experiences will define their purpose. You've got to love what you do. When you are younger, discover what that is and start there. Try everything and anything. Get out of your comfort zone. As they say, the world belongs to those who are doers—people who get things done. Doers don't just sit around and talk about their dreams and what they want to do, they GET IT DONE. Leverage every opportunity and explore any path. This will open doors and, ultimately, define your purpose.

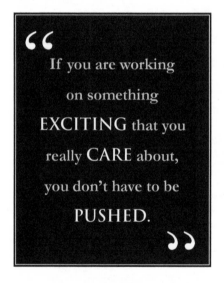

If you are working on something EXCITING that you really CARE about, you don't have to be PUSHED.

When you're passionate about what you're doing, it's not "work". Because I identified my "why" early in life, work never felt like a job and most days it was a hobby.

Switching gears toward those of us at a more mature stage in life, this approach may now be the opposite. After many years of experience, a journey of purpose will take us down other roads we never knew existed. Our purpose will start to define our passions.

Here's a nugget from coaching: When you know your purpose, your best years will always be right in front of you. This was as true for my 27-year career as it is a proven approach for young people. Whether passion or purpose leads the way, it comes down to this question for each of us: *Why do we do what we do?*

KNOWING YOUR WHY

As I entered my 12th year coaching in the Big Ten, I knew it was my last year. It was time. New athletic department leadership created many changes in the culture, and the resulting challenges made me feel disconnected from the institution I loved and represented.

Knowing this was my last year (nobody told me . . . I could just feel it), the department's leaders would ignore me in the hallway and walk the other way when they saw me. One administrator pretended to be on his cell phone every time I walked by or stopped by his office, cowardly. He didn't say a word or have the courage to look up at me. You know, and everyone else knows, and you're treated like you have the plague. I felt like our team was on our own island and it didn't matter what our jerseys said on the front or whose colors we wore. I was the captain of a ship whose rudder was intact, but it was the mothership that felt rudderless.

This was the work environment that surrounded me in my last two seasons. Passionate and purposeful work, with great leadership modeled around coaches and the student-athletes? NOT! It was time to re-evaluate what I was doing and to decide if my values still aligned with this organization and its direction.

So, I stepped back and approached this final coaching season with a different mindset and focus—I planned to have the time of my life with my players and staff. I would love them like never before. I let my guard down and loved, laughed, and truly had the time of my life with the people I spent more time with than my family. I learned that vulnerability is POWER and I felt more powerful than ever before. I intended to be present in the moment and to coach for the love of the game. I would enjoy every moment of the game I had loved since the fifth grade. I focused on having fun and embracing the people around me instead of obsessing over the outcomes.

This final year of coaching, leading, and building relationships was one of the most enjoyable that I have ever experienced. I thought I knew what my passion and purpose were before going into my final season, but that year I put an exclamation point on it. I became an ON POINT leader, able to easily define and communicate my passion and my purpose at this stage of my life.

I rediscovered what I always knew: that my passion and purpose have always been to develop people and push them to reach their full potential, as whole people. College athletics, basketball specifically, gave me the gift of that opportunity. Today, I am still exercising that purpose and passion, but now in a different venue with high-level business leaders and teams. It's a new challenge afforded me because of my success as a college basketball coach, and one that I relish every day.

GIVING YOUR HEART

In the locker room, board room, corner office, or front line, passion can be fueled and ignited in a team setting by creating an inspiring, shared vision. Developing an inspiring vision is the first critical step in sharing your passion. The ability to align your team and focus on success together—toward a destination and in a manner shared by the team—is the mark of a leader. Passion and purpose flourish when you enable your team to "give from the heart" to accomplish their shared goals.

Leading with the heart, as portrayed by legendary Duke men's basketball coach Mike Krzyzewski in his book of the same title, enables the deep relationships formed by a shared sense of purpose developed through the leader's relationship with the team. According to Coach K, "[a]lmost everything in leadership comes down to relationships. The only way you can possibly lead people is to understand people. And the only way you can understand people is to get to know them." My final season proved the true value, and great gift, that creating deep relationships could deliver.

I wonder what it would have been like to approach every year like I did my first few and my last? Loving, laughing, and having the time of my life with people who gave me everything they had every single day—their hearts and souls. We were focused on doing our very best instead of being consumed daily with the outcomes. All those years in-between, I was so consumed with winning on the court that I forgot what winning really meant in life. What more could we have accomplished with this shift in perspective?

Throughout this final year on the bench, I learned to block inside and outside influences from destroying my love, my passion, and my energy sources. I rediscovered that the leader's essential purpose is to create an environment and a culture where people want to work, play, and learn. Then, lead from the heart and from the soul, with all your might.

After 27 years on the bench, I tapped fully into this lesson in my last few seasons and it brought my role as an ON POINT leader into sharp focus. Most importantly, the deeply fulfilling relationships I built those years enriched my life and will always hold a special place in my heart. It turns out winning isn't about numbers on the scoreboard or record books . . . it's about people, relationships, purpose, and passion.

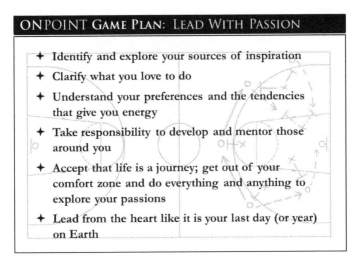

ON POINT GAME PLAN: LEAD WITH PASSION

+ Identify and explore your sources of inspiration
+ Clarify what you love to do
+ Understand your preferences and the tendencies that give you energy
+ Take responsibility to develop and mentor those around you
+ Accept that life is a journey; get out of your comfort zone and do everything and anything to explore your passions
+ Lead from the heart like it is your last day (or year) on Earth

BEING TRUE TO YOU

"To be yourself in a world that is constantly trying
to make you something else is the greatest accomplishment."
–Ralph Waldo Emerson–

What does it mean to be true to you? I've asked myself this hard question. Some people are branded by their looks, skillset, title, or position. These labels may be descriptive, but they poorly and incompletely define the essence of an individual.

To be true to yourself means acting in alignment with who you are and what you believe. If you know and love yourself, you will find it effortless to be true to yourself. Seek to define what is most important to you, and what values you hold sacred, then target your actions to fulfill those priorities.

Be who you are! Have the courage to accept yourself—the real you—not who someone else thinks you should be. Don't pretend to be someone else in order to gain approval, and don't struggle to change the essential fabric of you.

AUTHENTICITY

Many of my former collegiate players believed that doing things to please their peers, such as partying or behaving in inappropriate ways when the coaches were not watching, would bring them acceptance and approval. They acted against the expectations and values of their coaches and parents, and their own common sense, only to find themselves in trouble and underperforming on and off the court. Unfortunately, this was a common occurrence. Out of the reach of their parents, my players' behaviors and resulting underperformance were known only to me and my coaching staff. I faced an ongoing leadership challenge to help my players understand the consequences of their choices and to help them make choices that valued the team's success first.

When your behaviors and actions are not genuine, you won't be happy with yourself or looked at as someone who others want to follow. Self-respect comes from being true to who you really are—believing in yourself and living your values. People sense when leaders are strong and capable of standing up for their beliefs.

Once, I was the keynote speaker at an annual mother/daughter leadership and etiquette event at the St. Paul Hotel in Minneapolis. At the event I met a young woman who was a junior in high school. Everyone was dressed to the nines; they had their Sunday best on and I felt like I was at the prom. Everyone wore three-inch heels, bright lipstick, the best accessories, and gorgeous dresses. It was a long time since I'd attended the prom so I was soaking in the moment with the moms and their daughters.

My message to this audience was *Being True To You.* It was an emotional and empowering afternoon. The message was powerful and hearts were touched. After I finished speaking and the event concluded, a young woman maneuvered her way through the crowd where I was standing with some of the mothers and the organizers of the event. She tapped me on the shoulder and said, *Coach Pam, can I talk to you?* She was a beautiful, slender young woman.

I turned to her so I could directly face her and I said, *Of course.* She said, *Coach Pam, I was so touched by your message today and I want to ask you a question on how to deal with a situ-*

ation that has been bothering me for a year. I used to play basketball; it was my passion and I loved the game more than anything. One day in practice, my coach thought he was motivating me and told me that I was never going to be a good player or effective on the court. He told me I was too skinny, not tough enough, and needed more bulk to be able to push other girls around on the court. Those words hurt me. I can't help that I'm slender and built this way. He thought he was motivating me. Instead of showing me how to use my strengths, he tore me down. After the season was over, I quit playing the game I love . . . and I miss it.

> "A bird sitting on a tree is NEVER AFRAID of the branch breaking, because her TRUST is not on the branch but on her WINGS."
>
> –Unknown–

She had huge tears rolling down her cheeks as she told me this story. As I listened, my eyes filled with tears and after she finished, I asked if I could give her a hug and I told her that I believed in her. The coach's words affected her so much that they had been tearing her up for a year and drove her away from sports. She said, *Coach Pam, I want to go and talk to this coach and tell him this, but how do I have this hard conversation? Should I talk to him or just let it go?* I thought about her situation and responded, *Obviously, this is something that has bothered you and you can't let it go. You need to have this conversation so you can move on or you will regret it.*

For the next 10 minutes, I walked her through how to have this conversation with her former coach. We talked about being prepared and discussed the impact of her body language, her tone, and the words she chooses. She thanked me and we had one last hug (and a few more tears) together. Then, I watched the tall, beautiful, slender, and now confident young woman walk out of the banquet room. I smiled and couldn't take my eyes off of her, feeling great pride in this 17-year-old high school junior who just needed a little confidence and courage in order to move forward. I knew she would stay true to herself and aligned to her beliefs—she knew where she wanted to go in her life.

COURAGE, DOUBT, AND GRIT

Staying true to you takes courage. It requires self-reflection, sincerity, and open-mindedness. It does not mean that you must be selfish, inconsiderate, or disrespectful of others. It means that you won't let others define you.

Most of us need someone around to push us, to challenge us, and to hold us accountable. That's okay and it's constructive; we will talk more about that later in the book. In the end, it comes down to you, your attitude, and your ability to stay the course. Believing in yourself and having courage are rewarding and bring out the best in all of us. It did for me and it has changed my life.

We all can stay true to ourselves. It's a choice. This separates the very good from the extraordinary leaders. You can do more than you think you can in every way. Trust me, I know. I believe in myself and I believe in you, too!

Self-doubt is the enemy of staying true to you. Slaying self-doubt builds a powerful spirit and feeling of staying true to who you are. Gaining confidence and being empowered to believe in yourself must become one of your strengths.

Sometimes, circumstances challenge our self-belief, courage, and confidence. In these cases, you may have to rely on another important character trait: grit. When was the last time you showed true grit? Everyone has grit and has either demonstrated it at some point in their lives or it's living inside waiting to be released.

True grit is resilience, determination, and doing whatever it takes to accomplish something—while staying true to you. In our personal and professional lives, each of us faces adversity and must demonstrate grit to stay the course. We can choose to stay the course, doing what is right consistently, or choose to give in to an easier path of shortcuts or band-aid solutions. Your ability to persevere and to demonstrate the courage to believe in yourself are the deciding factors.

Be true to the very best that resides within you and live your life consistently with your highest values and integrity. Those who are most successful in life have dared to live this way and they look back and have no regrets. This is true for anyone in any profession. There are great leaders who never make it to the CEO's chair. There are great coaches who never make it to a Final Four. There are excellent leaders who make it to that chair and superior coaches who do experience a Final Four. Then, there are coaches and business leaders who choose to win at all costs, take shortcuts, cheat, and who do not do the right thing.

So, what did that mean for me? I wondered how I could stay true to myself while pursuing a career in competitive athletics where coaches never win enough, no accomplishment is ever good enough, players are never talented enough, and you're always second guessed by the experts. If you don't win enough or you can't sustain or grow the business fast enough, you will be replaced. How do you stay true to yourself, your values, and your beliefs when faced with these brutal expectations?

After the 2008 season, I did not stay true to what I believed. Faced with extreme pressure, I turned away from the right formula to sustain the program and to continue consistently reaching NCAA Tournaments every year. That season, we had a great regular season and it was one of the most rewarding to me as a coach. Then, we lost in the first round of the NCAA Tournament to the University of Texas.

Matchups make the difference for a program and institution, as they did for us at Minnesota, when you reach the highest level of competition like the NCAA Tournament. Player to player, top to bottom, these Texas Longhorn thoroughbreds were too much for us to overcome. Their team just ran us off the floor. Their players were bigger, faster, and stronger at every position.

After the game and the way we got beat, we took a long hard look at the types of players we had on the team. We decided that we needed to recruit a different type of player and athlete in order to go deeper in the NCAA Tournament. We modified the way we recruited and how we evaluated talent, and the types of players we brought into the program changed.

In the short term, it seemed like an action we had to take. In the end, it turned out to be one of the biggest mistakes I made and it set the program back. For two years, we brought in more talented players, but they were the wrong fit and our approach changed the trajectory of the program in the wrong way. In 2009, our temporary success didn't show us the error of our ways. We had a great year and upset Notre Dame on their home court in the first round of the NCAA Tournament, advancing to the second round. Unfortunately, our direction of recruiting had already changed with the class we had signed and we were heading down the wrong road. I did not stay true to what I believed in and the types of people and players that fit the University of Minnesota's culture, the Big Ten, my coaching style and values, and our program's sustainability.

In order to win, we recruited better athletes but we sacrificed the fit, values, skillset, discipline, team play, and character of individuals who wanted to be at Minnesota for all the right reasons. We needed players who would run through a wall, put the team first, and work harder than any team in the country. What we got was a collection of talented players we couldn't mesh and that clashed with our University, program, coaching, and team values.

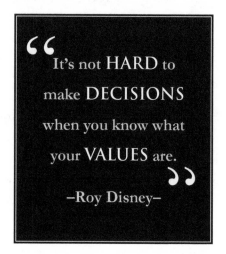

It's not HARD to make DECISIONS when you know what your VALUES are.

–Roy Disney–

I soon realized that I did not stay true to my values and beliefs. I learned that I needed to stay the course and believe in the people with whom I had surrounded myself in the first place when we were winning, graduating players, and representing the institution with class. There is nothing more important for business leaders and employers than to recruit, hire, and surround themselves with the right people. This is an art and will make or break you as a leader. I will talk more about this in detail in Chapter 7.

What does it take to be true to you? Why is this important? I want you to achieve your goals and dreams and I believe the answer lies in being true to yourself. An ON POINT leader who knows her true self, her values, and follows her true path can lead others to become their own true (and best) selves.

My years of experience have confirmed it for me. Those I've coached, players and clients, prove the undeniable connection between your values, character, and integrity with the ability to achieve greatness as an ON POINT leader. If you stay true to yourself and stay the course, challenges will work out the way they are supposed to . . . and opportunities for success will follow.

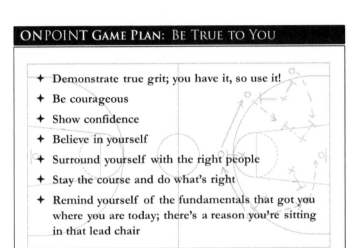

ON POINT GAME PLAN: BE TRUE TO YOU

+ Demonstrate true grit; you have it, so use it!
+ Be courageous
+ Show confidence
+ Believe in yourself
+ Surround yourself with the right people
+ Stay the course and do what's right
+ Remind yourself of the fundamentals that got you where you are today; there's a reason you're sitting in that lead chair

WINNING IS NEVER GOOD ENOUGH

"Winning isn't everything—but wanting to win is."
–Vince Lombardi–

In big-time college athletics, depending on who you are and what school you represent, you can never win enough games or even win by enough points. If you beat someone you're supposed to and it was a close game, the next day' social media posts, blogs, and newspaper articles would suggest that you lost the game.

We say in athletics that there are "ugly" wins. Sometimes you have to grind it out, like when you've played three Big Ten games in one week, when you play games on the road, and when you play games at the end of the season. Every sport has these types of games—they take willpower, grit, resilience, and an ability to find a way to get it done. But many fans, "experts" behind a computer, and sportswriters believe that winning this way is not good enough. Only coaches know that any win is a good win, and we will take a win however we can get it, any night, against any opponent. It doesn't matter how pretty it is . . . a win is a win. Coaches and players also understand that many people who sit in the stands are "armchair quarterbacks" and have their own ideas on how teams should win.

For them, winning is never good enough.

THE CURSE OF EXPECTATIONS

Here's a secret held by many head coaches in major-college athletics: they love practice and dislike games. In practice, coaches can focus on the process. They can instruct and inspire their team members, stopping the action to highlight a great play or to correct a misstep. They can work with the whole team and manage all of its parts, together, as a cohesive unit. They can remove distractions and diversions to immerse themselves in the aspects of the game they love.

But game time always looms, and the pressures and expectations have changed. The stakes today are very different from 10 to 15 years ago in major-college athletics in almost every sport. Winning is everything and it comes down to who you are working for, your boss, the score, your record, and consistent post-season appearances. April to November is the favorite time of the year for many basketball coaches—the time when they develop their team, build relationships with players, and plan for the impending season. You would be surprised at how many coaches have said this out loud. I've had coaches tell me five minutes before the tip-off, at Big Ten meetings, and on recruiting trips, that they dislike games because there is too much pressure to win every one. Coaches are vulnerable with each other because few people know and can relate to this feeling.

You may be surprised to hear this because you're supposed to look forward to games. The fans certainly do, but for the coach, their spouse, and family it's just a vicious cycle, because simply winning the game is never good enough for people outside the arena walls. I had a sportswriter who would write the ugliest columns in the paper—and never attended even one of my games.

Coaching is very lonely. The major-college coach understands that winning is never good enough unless you win the national championship and are nearly undefeated. That's the life of the major-college coach. The season produces excruciating pressure and such a high stress level that one needs to change their mindset and perspective to have fun and to provide a good experience for all.

It's true; coaches feel that they need to win every game and this is how most operate on a daily basis. Because of this condition, the expectations and stress level of the players is also higher than it's ever been. They feel it top-down from the coaching staff and from every angle: the fans, social and traditional media, parents, friends, and themselves. Today, it is common for athletic departments to employ full-time sports psychologists on staff. Their schedules are booked dealing with the endless challenges and issues that student-athletes face today. Student-athlete well-being is where resources are needed the most.

Winning is never good enough.

DEFINING VICTORY

So, what does winning look like to you? Of course the wins were very important and, at one point in my career, they were all that mattered to me. All I focused on was winning. That's what everyone talked about on the outside on social media, in blogs, and everywhere I went. I was consumed with winning and losing. It controlled me and was what I focused on, constantly.

During my first three years at Minnesota, we won 25 games each season and we went to consecutive Sweet 16s and the program's first-ever Final Four. After that run, the bar was set even higher and framed the expectations every season for a long time. This type of success does not happen at a school like Minnesota every year. Most national schools can only experience a certain level of success and only a handful of schools can sustain such success year after year. The University of Minnesota is not one of those places. It was incredibly hard to get this program to a Final Four, and it was even harder to sustain it.

MY WINNING DEFINITION

Winning integrates character, honesty, trust, integrity and teamwork in developing the best people and teams possible. Winning means my people and teams have a great experience, I create a healthy environment, I graduate players, I grow a business, I instill resilience and work ethic, I exercise discipline, and I develop future leaders. Winning is watching my team members excel and experience success.

Have you experienced any or all of this? I have experienced it all, and it is how I define winning!

The competitive environment is characterized by a mindset of "what have you done for me lately." People don't have patience for the process, to build a solid foundation, and they want you to win NOW. Despite the accomplishments, no one cares what you did in the past. In an instant gratification world, the focus is on the next win and at any point can be left behind for the next exciting job, coach, or event.

In big-time college athletics, the need to spend money to win in football and basketball is an arms race. You can never win enough and the more you win, the more money is spent. Expectations rise higher and higher, and the slope gets steeper and more dangerous. What does winning look like for you?

In 2002, when I took over the University of Minnesota women's basketball program, the entire operation was a mess. When I say the entire operation, I mean the entire operation including the athletic department. Some of the nation's best coaches toiled under the roof in the Bierman Field Athletic Building, but the leadership and business model was changing.

In the women's basketball program, a number of NCAA violations had occurred prior to my arrival and the program was facing stiff penalties. When I took the job, the penalties were unknown. When the NCAA finished their investigation and handed out our penalties, they included the loss of a few weeks of practice time, elimination of some scholarships for two years, and one fewer coach on the road for recruiting.

Winning was never good enough. What price are you willing to pay in order to win? What lines are you willing to cross to win?

Handcuffed, we went to work. Blessed with talent, a bit of luck, and the right systems in place we exceeded expectations. Here's what we did: first, we established that there was more to our team than the objective of winning. On a scale of 1 to 10, winning ranked an 8.5. We reserved a 10 for respect, the process, relationship building, academics, and trust. We were ON POINT from the beginning and there was no looking back.

True, winning is never good enough. The previous coach left after one season for a better situation and job—after the team had experienced its best season in many years, won 22 games, and advanced to the second round of the NCAA Tournament. And it still wasn't good enough.

☸

For now, accept that winning is only the start of the journey for an ON POINT leader. But, know that winning will never be enough. So, NOW how would you define winning in business and in your life? Will you work only for wins and losses, or will you abandon that zero-sum game and find deeper, more meaningful ways to play?

ONPOINT GAME PLAN: DEFINE WINNING

+ Build an authentic, honest, and healthy mindset about winning
+ Define what is important to you
+ Establish a clear picture of your values
+ Recognize how you make people feel, in good times and bad
+ Clarify what price you are willing to pay to win
+ Ask yourself: *Have I given my best effort?*
+ Know that if you focus only on wins, you will experience frequent loss
+ Accept the things you can control, and release those you cannot

THE EXPERTS

"You'll be judged. Keep going."
–Unknown–

The world is a complex, evolving place that changes every moment of every day. The hyper-speed flow of information is daunting. The positives, negatives, and unknowns are constant. We are seeing a monumental shift towards user-generated virtual content and people listen to this chatter, relying on it to inform their opinions, beliefs, and choices. In fact, it's often trusted more than traditional informational sources. But it's not vetted and it's not authenticated; the sources are people who most of us in athletics call *the experts.*

TURNING THE OTHER CHEEK

For more than a decade, I was a popular topic of conversation in many mediums and forums: social media, television, radio, newsprint, the office water cooler, campus watering holes, and many other places. Can you imagine? I have read hundreds of comments from the experts who thought they were ON POINT . . . at least they thought so. I read some of the most stomach-turning comments about my players, incoming recruits, my staff, how we should play, play calling and substitutions, pace of play—anything you can imagine about the team and its operations. To top it off, opinions commonly addressed my personal situations: how I should have been fired every year and comments about my contract, my personal life, my partner, and my friends. It was unreal. Hurtful. Disgusting. Mean. Personal. Attacking.

I guarantee this type of faceless, baseless criticism is happening in your world, too. One of my clients emailed me recently and vented about how a blog site was bashing her company, trashing her leadership, and trying to put them out of business. Another client texted me about a social media post about her and how it was affecting her daughter. Your critics may not be as public as mine or those of these clients, but don't be surprised if they are firing off opinions in the hallways, meeting rooms, and email streams where you work and live.

What should we do? As a community, we need to rally and fight against the systematic demeaning of others. There are many people who enjoy hurting others. They are unhappy, insecure, and jealous of other people's success. They are dissatisfied with how their own lives play out and they take joy in hurting others. Cowardly sitting behind a computer with little or no accountability, they write hurtful messages and words and then click send or post. It's sad that this makes them feel better, powerful, and in control. Do you know someone like this? Have you done this before?

If you're a parent, I'm sure you are experiencing similar situations daily, as your children navigate the untethered world of online communication. If you're a kid, this is cyber-bulling at its worst. As a business leader, your decisions are being questioned often. As a coach, the experts feel that it's open game, it comes with the territory, and it's part of the job. In fact, they feel obligated in some twisted way. We have all experienced this at some level—the experts invite themselves in and ransack our lives. This type of behavior has shattered people's lives, families, livelihoods, and friendships.

I've seen such degrading behavior on my athletic teams and in teams I coach in business. This is a norm in middle school and high school, from the parents and especially from *the experts*—the media and fans. By now you have a pretty good picture of *the experts:* fans in the stands, people behind computer screens, the media and, in some cases, perhaps you.

There are blogs, forums, apps, and websites in our industries and communities we can visit and read the most hurtful messages and opinions from people. I would always (and often) tell my staff, players, my own parents, and my partner to stay off the blogs. I would plead with them not to read the nonsense and the comments at the end of the editorial columns online or the articles in the paper. My assistant coach was funny and believed that the more he read them, the stupider he got. That's how crazy people are—*the experts.* Each comment was further and further from the truth and words were used that no person would ever say to someone's face. To describe this situation as passive-aggressive is an understatement.

The further I got into my career—a veteran, more confident and an ON POINT leader secure in my own skin, experiencing a tremendous amount of success— these comments from *the experts* actually became entertaining. I wonder if *the experts* actually knew we were being entertained. Who has that much time to spend behind a computer saying hurtful things?

Can you imagine how *the expert's* mind works, what they spend their time thinking about, and how making other people's lives miserable consumes them? These people have not accomplished what they thought they would in their own lives. Even those who are paid to render opinions, like the media, often went beyond the realm of acceptable, responsible commentary; I often pondered how their athletic experience, or conditions of upbringing, contributed to their negativity.

Most of the population takes these harsh and untrue acts to heart. They subject themselves to these sites and read comments that are destructive to their confidence, customers, business, and families. We've got to turn this around and stop giving these people a platform. This negativity creates destruction of people and communities—even as drastic as suicide or violence toward others. The everyday person usually isn't strong enough to handle the negativity and public nature of these forums. Believing the talk is true, this type of trash metaphorically, and sometimes literally, takes people down to their knees and shutters them in their homes, afraid to face their friends and coworkers who may have read it.

Social media demands a lot of our time on top of our already demanding lives. So, let's disconnect, as we need to, and renew our outside interests and refresh ourselves. Don't read it. Believe in yourself and what you're doing. There is a reason why you're the target. Look around; I'll bet it's because you're talented, you're successful, you've received a scholarship, you're accomplished, and you're living a great life. Dismiss the noise and get involved in activities to lead people to a place of harmony and teamwork.

Don't allow yourself to get caught up in the negative energy of the social media space. Believe me and my former assistant coach, it just makes you stupid. And you're not! It takes courage, resilience, self-belief, and the right people and team surrounding you.

KEEPING YOUR CHIN UP

I've highlighted the harm others can cause you, but what if the shoe is on the other foot? Remember, what happens on social media stays in cyberspace forever. If you are the one to click send or post, you can be held accountable, always. It all has the power to make the innocent guilty and to make the guilty innocent. But it only has that power if you allow it.

Keep your chin up. Be powerful and courageous by not being *the expert* and clicking the send or post button. You're ON POINT in your own life and that takes strength and courage. I applaud you. Join me and practice how I dealt with *the experts'* nonsense. First, have confidence in what you're doing. Look at what you're doing, and take stock of where you are in your life and what you have accomplished. Be the bigger person, take the high road, and be a leader!

Many times the fans in the stands were not on my side; some of the people around you may be rooting against you. But every time, I was professional and I accepted that the naysayers came with the territory. The things I heard, saw, and felt from *the experts* were tough, but I was laser-focused as a coach and always stayed between the four lines on the court. The experts motivated me every day and it fueled my fire. The more that I was told I couldn't do it, the harder I pushed, becoming even more driven. I learned to turn the negative energy and those people into my inspiration. I dismissed their criticism as nonsense and didn't let it in. You can do this, too!

True, all of this comes with the territory for a head coach in big-time college athletics. But my family, friends, and especially my partner were also subject to the brutal comments in the stands. Toward the end of my career at the University of Minnesota, I told my partner, Lynn, that she didn't need to attend my home games. Winning wasn't enough for *the experts* anymore. My loyal friends, my family and, particularly, Lynn were subject to "amateur hour" frequently at the games. I understand Minnesota's Williams Arena had the best ice cream at the concession stand, but I would never know because for 12 years I never had any. I left as soon as the game and press conference concluded. The arena lost any sense of "sweetness" for me as she came under attack.

One game, Lynn stood in line at half-time and a woman (why is it always women who put other women down?) approached her and said, *This is disgusting basketball.* Another time Lynn was in the bathroom and a woman walked up as she washed her hands, stood beside her, and said, *She [Pam] deserves to be fired.* Lynn was subject to everything and, for the spouse or partner, it is always harder than for the coach. The coach can focus on the team and the game. The spouse or partner has no control and no recourse; they want to do something to help but can't.

It was agonizing . . . she couldn't get away from *the experts* in the stands or escape from the media. People sat near her and would talk loud enough for her to hear their negative comments about coaching decisions, about how the kids were playing, and so on. I was furious to learn about these attacks. Come on, really? Does that make you feel better to stab a knife into someone's heart and soul, and to shatter someone who is hurting for her partner? It's a game. They're kids.

I learned the most important lessons going through some of the most difficult times you could ever imagine. Most importantly, I learned to surround myself with the right people: those who love you, support you, and protect you no matter what. If you are in the midst of a difficult period, circle the wagons, keep your inner circle small, and stay visible and relevant—it's very powerful and inspiring for people to see you when things are not going well. When you stand up in the midst of the storm, strong and steady, you show the world your character and your determination.

I also learned to repeat a powerful thought to myself, to my friends, and to my family: social media and traditional media never really know the full story, so their opinions are inherently flawed from the beginning. If you are the person behind the story, living in the story, you know this as fact. In my case as a coach, there were challenges and issues that occurred daily with 18- to 22-year-old young adults. At times, putting the ball in the basket didn't seem to be the most important thing in the face of daily challenges that varied every day. My perspective of what it meant to be an ON POINT coach and leader—beyond the wins and losses—helped me learn this lesson.

A life-changing time event for me as a coach solidified this learning. One evening, a player came to me requesting I attend counseling with her. Of course I agreed, and I was humbled with the level of trust that came with her request. I was proud of our strong relationship, but I didn't know what need the counseling would address. It turned out to be for a tragedy: a childhood laced with sexual abuse. I was there for her and basketball was secondary. I worked with her and other young adults on the court and in the locker room, but my primary responsibility was for their personal health and development. I was in charge of helping shape their lives and development as players AND people once their parents sent them off to college.

How could the media have known of this tragic backstory? They couldn't. Of course her on-court performance would be affected. Remember this the next time you're reading a dramatic news account. Most likely, you don't have the real facts or the whole story. Don't put all your trust into *the experts*.

One of the many responsibilities of an ON POINT leader is to know how to handle *the experts* in your industry who are negative and are trying to take you down. This is easy to talk about, but extremely difficult to experience and to handle with grace. You've got to take the high road every time and understand that those who sit behind a computer and click send or post just don't matter. Keep your chin up.

Dealing with and owning the "lonely chair" of a leader just can't be taught but can be learned; you learn it and earn it on the job. When you achieve that high-level position you've been seeking, when you're at the top, you will understand the loneliness. You will need to figure out whom to trust, to find out who really understands, and to discover who will be there through thick and thin. You'll find the people who support you through the good and the bad. Surprisingly, you'll find your greatest supporters mostly through the bad.

When you make the big time it's not as easy and glamorous as everyone thinks. And, you'll find that many want the lofty position, but really can't handle the pressure and expectations that come with it. Do you really want to sit in that chair? Do your co-workers? *The experts* think they can sit there, but I truly believe they would rather sit behind their computers or in the stands. When and if you get there, you'll need resilience, perseverance, and self-belief like never before. Everyone around you will question, second-guess, try to take you down, and think they can do it better.

There will also come a point, if you want to succeed, when you will need to embrace the position. If you surround yourself with good people, people who are smarter and more talented than you are, you will begin to rise above. Accept the challenges of the "lonely chair" and build a resilient, supportive team.

Drown out the noise of *the experts* who are really just driving destructive negativity. Don't read it and, most importantly, don't respond. Stand strong and firm in your conviction in the performance you will achieve and in the integrity of your character. Quite frankly, the only true experts I know are my parents.

When you reach the leadership position and the level of success you want, you must understand that your worth is not measured in likes, comments, awards, notes, or followers. Who cares?! Keep your chin up, stay true to yourself, and make sure you're the one who is ON POINT in your own life—not *the experts*.

ONPOINT GAME PLAN: SURVIVE THE EXPERTS

+ Don't get caught up with social media, blogs, forums, and their negativity . . . don't respond
+ If you subject yourself to reading it, be the bigger person and take the high road
+ Don't take it personally; believe in yourself
+ Help your kids understand the truth about the experts; stay the course
+ Circle the wagons and surround yourself with the right people: those who love you, support you, and protect you no matter what
+ Stay visible and relevant

FIRED

"My past has not defined me, destroyed me, deterred me, or defeated me; it has only strengthened me."
—Dr. Steve Maraboli—

You never leave high-powered positions the way you dreamed you would. My departure from the University of Minnesota wasn't how I wrote the script. It wasn't how I imagined I'd leave after 12 years—just quietly ushered out the door. No fanfare, no gold watch, no rocking chair retirement ceremony.

I was in an unhealthy and dysfunctional situation at the University of Minnesota toward the end of my career, but getting fired wasn't my first choice. In 2014, at the age of 48, this was a first for me. I was suddenly set adrift and needed to chart a new course in life.

Even though I knew it was coming for two years, I prepared as much as I could and steeled myself for how it would feel when it actually happened. I was the winningest coach in program history and had a Final Four, three Sweet 16s, and multiple NCAA Tournaments under my belt. I had one of the top NCAA post-season records for Big Ten coaches at 9 wins, 6 losses. But, what I did then didn't matter now. It was more like: *What have you done for me lately?*

THE LAST STAND

We had rebuilt the program with talented players who were future WNBA draft picks. The program was back to where it could and should be. Going into the 2012-2013 season, I was told if I didn't make the NCAA Tournament, the University would change leadership. A tournament berth was the only thing that mattered to the new leadership. To top it off, I wasn't the new athletic director's selected coach or hire; they inherited me. I believed I was a goner from day one.

When the season ended, they fired Tubby Smith, the men's head basketball coach, instead. Tubby is an established legend in college basketball. He is regarded in the profession as one of the most respected and dynamic coaches in the game. At the University of Kentucky, he coached the Wildcats to the 1998 National Championship. In his final season at Minnesota, his team achieved the program's first non-probation NCAA victory since 1990. He'd led the program to its best season in 22 years . . . then he was fired. A few years after his Minnesota firing, Tubby was named 2016 Big 12 Coach of the Year at Texas Tech and received the 2016 John R. Wooden Legends of Coaching Award.

Tubby's firing was a lesson in how not to do things, especially in a very visible and public arena. Athletics is a window into the University and, in this case, everyone in the nation watched how the situation unfolded. There wasn't a communication plan in place and the conduct of the University was an embarrassment, full of disrespect, and a disgrace to a great man whose character, integrity, and professionalism were unassailable.

Every coach in America, no matter the sport, has a tremendous amount of respect for Tubby Smith. With the way the decision broke and proceeded, it would be extremely tough to hire another basketball coach. There was no plan to roll out the decision to let him go; the University didn't identify who would share the message, what message points to emphasize, and when and where to break the news. It was an absolute embarrassment.

The decision to fire Tubby was a fait accompli and both the president's office and the Board of Regents had been told already. Somehow, this information leaked to the press and the news of Tubby getting fired was on ESPN's sports-ticker and the local news before Tubby knew himself. This was a major communication breakdown from the top down—and considering the speed at which information travels, and not knowing who to tell or not to tell, the University caused a firestorm.

For the remaining Minnesota coaches and many others in the department, the situation was another sign of how business would proceed under the new leadership. Planning, communication, trust, and respect are fundamental attributes of leadership at every level; the decision and its execution put many of us on notice that these basic attributes were lacking in our new leadership.

Tubby's name was scrolling across EPSN's sports-ticker at the bottom of the television screen and his phone was ringing off the hook before the athletic director gave him the news. Tubby didn't believe it—he had just engineered the best season in the program in 22 years, so why would he think he would get fired? He was asked to vacate the building that day and his office belongings and boxes would be delivered to his house.

I'm sure if everyone had the opportunity to do this again, it would have been handled completely different. Every coach and student-athlete in the department watched this unfold; hundreds of athletes, staff, coaches, and University employees were affected. We all watched the situation closely and for many of us, there was no better mentor and role model than Tubby. We recognized what type of atmosphere lay ahead for the rest of the staff and department—and it proved to be true.

After the decision and ensuing debacle, I was positive they would walk down the hallway and fire me next. But, for some reason, I was "spared" for another year. Unfortunately, that gratuitous year was like waiting on a guillotine for a year, knowing the fatal outcome. My staff and players had to grind through the season and make the best of it with people we all cared about. I led the way with our vision, set goals, got everyone on board, and executed the game plan throughout the year. I was ON POINT as usual and really had to be in this fragile, pressure-cooker situation. We were a family and we carried on with business as usual, went to battle on game day, and acted like everything was going to be OK.

THE FINAL SEASON

Heading into the 2013-2014 season, I knew it would be my last year whether we qualified for the NCAA Tournament or not. Tubby's experience had made it crystal clear what the future held. As the season started it was apparent; I was ignored and marginalized. I was invisible to our leadership because that was the manner in which they functioned. For eight months, my staff and I were treated without professionalism and respect and we felt disconnected from the University of Minnesota.

Can you imagine being told your job was on the line, then preparing for another brutal Big Ten season, and knowing your livelihood depended on a group of fragile 18- to 22-year-olds? My players and staff knew the tenuous situation; I never told them but they knew. I had the hardest-working, most connected, and loyal staff I have ever put together. I was lucky to be surrounded by such great people and friends. Our team gave us their heart and souls and they played every game, every minute, and every day for our jobs. We were their role models and mentors, and they had great relationships with their coaches. They honored us with their tenacity on and off the court.

I felt their anguish after our losses and we celebrated our successes. I will never forget the looks on their faces and I will always remember that they gave everything they had. At the conclusion of the regular season, we watched the Monday Madness NCAA Tournament selection show together as a team. We were a "bubble team," sitting on the outside looking in with 20 wins and a strong Rating Percentage Index (RPI) strength-of-schedule ranking.

The team huddled together in the locker room during the ESPN announcement of tournament teams and seedings. When our name wasn't called, the players looked at me with tears in their eyes, their shoulders sagged and heads dropped, and they looked at one another. The room was silent and the air was heavy. I walked into the hallway with my senior women's administrator and we looked at each other with tears rolling down our cheeks. She hugged me and said she was so sorry. We all knew what that announcement meant.

Our post-season, and the last days of my coaching career, consisted of playing in the WNIT as long as we could. We had played the season, fighting as long and hard as we could, with just seven healthy players. Day after day, game after game, for five months I continued to look down the bench but found no bench strength—our well was dry. Yet, despite our struggles, I couldn't have been more proud of this team. This group of strong, resilient, young women will always be special to me and hold a special place in my heart.

We entered the WNIT with a mix of defiance and gratefulness, taking a nail-biting victory over Green Bay, 62-60, in the first round. After dispatching Southern Methodist University 77-70 in the second round, we traveled to South Dakota with a berth in the WNIT quarterfinals at stake. We played with grit and grim determination and pushed ourselves up to and past our physical and emotional limits. Unfortunately, our run as a team, and mine as the coach, came to an unceremonious end with a 70-62 loss.

It was a long bus ride home from South Dakota and I sat in my seat and just stared out the window. Lynn, my partner, had attended every game in this final year, knowing it would be the last time she watched me coach from the sidelines for the school we both loved. As we made the long bus ride home, she was just one of the many thoughts on my mind.

My players were in the back, my staff was all around me, and we were a family on our last ride home together. Nothing prepares you for something like this— no amount of planning, mentoring, or imagining can simulate the stark reality. The end, with a firing looming, was nothing short of a goat rodeo. My mind turned over the situation, assailed with terms like fired, terminated, released, dumped. I decided that "fired" might not be the best terminology for my emotional state. To wrap my mind around an event like this, "let go" felt like a more apt description.

I was very happy at Minnesota; it was a passion and never felt like a job until my last two years. Through a decade at the same institution and with the same athletic director, I was part of a healthy culture characterized by good leadership, a great support system, open communication, and mentoring. My values were aligned with those of the institution and the department. I had great mentors and an athletic director as boss who coached and developed coaches—exactly what coaches look for when they take a job. The department took pride in developing people; this is what they were supposed to do.

In major-college athletics, a coach has a typical shelf-life of five to seven years. Today, it could be less because of the unrealistic expectations that society, alumni, and fans put on winning. After a string of NCAA Tournament appearances, I had opportunities to leave. The grass was likely not greener somewhere else and I was committed and loyal to the University, to the community, and to the state of Minnesota. I had signed a new seven-year contract in 2010 after we upset Notre Dame on their home court in the NCAA Tournament, and I expected to fulfill it.

Before I signed the contract, my former athletic director called and told me I needed to leave Minnesota. For more than an hour, the topic of conversation centered on leaving while you're on top, the shelf-life of a coach, and the longevity in the profession. I listened intently and completely understood what he was saying, but I wasn't leaving my home and my program.

Other mentors, athletic directors, and close friends encouraged me to leave because they also understood the profession. But I was willing to take my chances; I just wanted to be happy where I lived and with the friends who surrounded me. In most cases, especially in men's basketball, constantly moving from one school to another is the formula for staying in the brutal profession until a coach becomes a pioneer. I didn't take the advice; I stayed and I ignored the search firms and agents.

A University, and especially the athletics program, is constantly in flux. It was in flux since day one when I accepted the job, until 12 years to the day when I was officially fired. Why did they hire me? I was told I was authentic; I represented a good fit with the community and people, I was a team player, and the team's star player endorsed me. I wasn't their first choice, but I was the coach who said yes. Their first choice turned them down, the second choice wanted more money, and I was next in line. I wanted the job and I wanted to be at Minnesota and to coach in the Big Ten more than anything.

Why did I take the job when no one else wanted it? For me, it was a great opportunity. It was coaching in the Big Ten and I was back in the Midwest where I grew up. There was some talent in the program and they had proven they could win. I didn't hesitate when they made the offer and I accepted the job over the phone. I didn't even ask about the salary. The only question I asked was about the duration of the contract. They offered me a five-year contract, with a good salary, but there was much more to the job than the money. It was about the opportunity and the potential, and I only wanted to coach a program with the resources and ability to reach the NCAA Final Four in New Orleans.

In 2012, the momentum was swinging back to the "golden years." I assembled a good staff, I had the right players, and we created a culture that was conducive to win again, consistently, at the University of Minnesota. Then, one of the worst things happened: my mentor, the athletic director, announced his retirement. I knew in my heart that the department would never be the same. He had built significant credibility and relationships with the student-athletes and coaches; he was a mentor, leader, and developer of people. There was a ripple effect throughout the department and we braced ourselves for adversity, change, and for some, a new chapter.

The search for the retiring athletic director's replacement was arduous. Many experienced and credible athletic directors were uninterested, withdrew from the process, or turned down job offers. The position was a risk to many experienced candidates because we had a new and unproven University president. The local media was vicious, unfair, and critical of the University—of course, they were *the experts* (see Chapter 5).

The first time I met the new athletic director was when he visited campus for the interview process. We weren't scheduled to meet; he was on a tour of the athletic complex and we just happened to cross paths. The person escorting him recognized me and introduced us. My first impression was that of a used car salesman in a wrinkled suit. His executive presence was lacking and, perhaps, he appeared out of his league and maybe in over his head.

He was traveling, probably tired, and drinking through a firehose in a new role. I should give him a break, but I won't—it's my book and it was my perspective. Fair or not, I got a sense with that first impression that he wondered why he was stopping to be introduced to the women's basketball head coach. He seemed uncomfortable being around me and, given what I now know, he was running away from a situation at his former school with his women's basketball coach. It now makes sense, but for whatever reason at that time, without the benefit of hindsight, I immediately felt it was going to be uncomfortable for him to be around confident and successful women.

Nearly instantly, the department's leadership and management model morphed to that of an outdated, 1950s-era command-and-control approach. The leadership style was coldly corporate and people were kept at arm's-length. It was loud and clear that building relationships with coaches and student-athletes wasn't part of the game plan. The top-down leadership approach characterized a model that would be considered destructive, short-sighted, and single-minded in businesses today.

To offset this approach, it became important for me to try and manage up and to build a relationship with him. I stopped by the new administration offices periodically to say hello. One administrator never got up from his chair and the other administrator kept the door closed or, ironically, always seemed to be on the phone (or pretending he was on the phone). I was hoping for an authentic, genuine mentor with high emotional intelligence, just like before. It hit me early on that my hope was a pipe dream. After 10 years, I was starting over.

Still, I committed to managing up and desperately wanted to establish a solid relationship, knowing it was my best strategy. I knew it wouldn't be easy, and it wasn't. My last two years, my new boss visited my office just once—on the day he fired me. He considered himself a basketball expert and guru, and clearly wanted to put his stamp on both basketball programs by hiring his own coaches.

THE DECISION

We'd been on the NCAA bubble each of my last two years. Things happen for a reason and it was time to go. After our WNIT loss to South Dakota, our bus rolled back into campus at 3:00 a.m. The following day I arrived at my office at 11:00 a.m. and my cell phone rang. The administration wanted to meet with me at 1:30 p.m. I knew what was going to happen in that meeting, and was relieved that it was Friday.

During the intervening two-and-a-half hours, two of my players stopped by, two assistants arrived at the office, and I called Lynn. I learned from my players that the administration had scheduled a team meeting at 3:30 p.m. I was the only person in the past 12 years who ever called a team meeting. The players asked what it was about and I told them the truth. Lynn booked two plane tickets to get out of town to visit our good friends' house in Arizona. Finally and mercifully, the meeting time arrived.

During the meeting, I was thanked for the blood, sweat, and tears I had poured into the program—and was informed that they needed to make a change in leadership. They told me to take my time cleaning out my office; I could do it at my leisure, in no hurry. They offered an on-campus office to use during my transition, if I needed one. I appreciated the respect they showed for all I did during my tenure at the University.

I had prepared for this moment for two years. I knew the time was coming. I thought I was prepared, but I wasn't, and tears rolled down my cheeks. The words, *we are going to make a change in leadership,* were the hardest and harshest words I'd heard in my life. This was MY program. I built it and rebuilt it three times over the course of 12 years. This program was my life, my players were my daughters, and the University is where I spent my life for more than a decade—building, molding, and nurturing a team to make the University, the students and alumni, and all Minnesotans proud. It was MY leadership they wanted to change, and I wasn't ready for the full emotional, personal impact of the decision.

They exercised my buy-out clause, releasing me from the two years left in my contract. The athletic director was in my office for only a couple of minutes; he left and the human resources administrator came in next. The press release had already been drafted; they showed me the press release, which they planned to release immediately, and asked if I wanted to add to it. I added a few sentences to the release and called Lynn and read it to her. We both approved it and I sent it back to them. Then I closed the door to my office. It was over.

We immediately left for Arizona and literally disappeared for five days. We went off the grid and left the media and people of the Twin Cities to spout off rumors, circulate vicious comments, and engage in any other drama that would unfold. This is typical; a few days of frenzy usually result from a change in a highly visible position like mine. Athletics is the window into most universities and the people in and around the University were getting a good look inside.

Getting fired was straightforward; it was simply a culmination of the process that had taken place over the last two years. It was the process and experience as I reconstruct the culture, the decisions, and the actions that tell the real story.

For two years, the department's leadership and communication style was one of absence and avoidance. My team and program were banished to an island and disconnected. Without support, we felt like we were representing the name on the back of the jersey, not the one on the front. As I look back now, my firing was a blessing and gift that freed me from further exposure to this toxic culture, leadership, and environment. Why couldn't anyone else see the damage caused by this environment and address its faults?

My experience is a cautionary story for leaders, informing them how not to treat their people and how quickly culture can shift. A culture of fear was created and everyone responded by looking out only for his or herself. A culture of family, collaboration, and high morale—a positive environment that took a dozen or more years to build—was quickly converted into an atmosphere lacking trust and forcing creation of silos to ensure survival. People operated within a climate of uncertainty; in this situation, only the eventual failure was certain.

THE COMEBACK

Things happen for a reason; I have always looked at life as if the glass were half full. My greatest strength, perhaps also my top weakness, is that I am an overly optimistic person. Belief is my number one strength, according to Tom Rath's book, *Strengths Finder*. Being able to let go was hard, and I understand the reasons, but the lessons I experienced and learned about leadership and how to respect and treat people are invaluable.

Over a year later, some in the Minnesota community still think I'm the coach and everyone still calls me Coach. How you leave doesn't determine if you are successful or not, but your body of work does. It's how you are able to change lives and make a difference that matter. The struggle I experienced at the end of my basketball coaching career made me stronger, more resilient, and a better leader and coach. The firing started a new chapter in my life and opened new doors that I would have never known before. Over the course of my career, I've learned to embrace adversity and demonstrate grace under fire (see Chapter 1) on many occasions. I am in an entirely new world that has given me so many gifts.

The way you leave is more important than how you arrive—especially if you are ever in a situation where it's not your choice to leave. Leave with grace, class, and dignity. You will always be remembered by how you leave and the integrity and character you embody. Everyone is watching. This will come back to you in many positive ways, because people will never forget how you made them feel.

Until leaving the University of Minnesota, my life experienced continuous upward movement. Suddenly, I found myself in a position with no direction or a plan. The slate was clean. My day-to-day schedule for the past 27 years was no longer defined. Was this what freedom felt like? Whether or not I felt free, the unstructured time was a gift and an opportunity.

I took time to stop, reflect, pause, and re-identify my purpose in life. It didn't take long because I idle high—no one had to shake me out of a listless funk or drag me off the couch. As I reflected on my path, I realized that I always knew my purpose and passion. It was time to continue my journey; my purpose and passion had never wavered in the past 27 years because it was always about people. Immediately, I knew that developing leaders, people, and teams in business and taking them to the next level would be my next chapter in life.

I left the University of Minnesota behind. I was right about the culture but took no real pleasure in the final resolution. On Friday, August 7, 2015, the athletic director who'd fired me resigned amid a number of alleged unethical actions. It was a sad day for a university I love. Chip Scoggins' editorial in the *Minneapolis Star-Tribune* two days later framed the discussion on the departing athletic director appropriately: "The best athletic directors are able to prioritize without alienating. To make everyone believe in a greater goal, even if they're not treated the same. In that regard, he failed miserably as a leader."

Today, I'm committed and determined to take successful leaders and teams to the next level. Developing effective leaders and coaching dysfunctional teams into high-performing ones is my expertise. I know what mark I will leave on this world, personally and professionally. I understand and embrace my legacy. I am ON POINT.

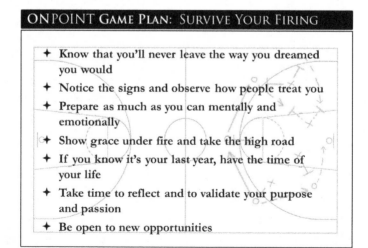

ONPOINT GAME PLAN: SURVIVE YOUR FIRING

+ Know that you'll never leave the way you dreamed you would
+ Notice the signs and observe how people treat you
+ Prepare as much as you can mentally and emotionally
+ Show grace under fire and take the high road
+ If you know it's your last year, have the time of your life
+ Take time to reflect and to validate your purpose and passion
+ Be open to new opportunities

PART TWO

DEVELOP A TEAM WITH THE RIGHT MIX OF SKILLS AND ATTITUDES

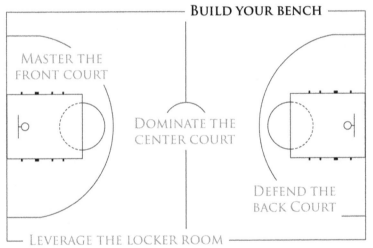

BUILD YOUR BENCH

MASTER THE
FRONT COURT

DOMINATE THE
CENTER COURT

DEFEND THE
BACK COURT

LEVERAGE THE LOCKER ROOM

RECRUITING, MOTIVATING, AND RETAINING TOP TALENT

"Hard work beats talent when talent doesn't work hard."
—Tom Notke—

One of the most common leadership maxims is to surround your-self with the right teammates. My coaching career—recruiting talent and hiring program staff—brought home the critical importance of assessing, selecting, developing, and retaining the right team.

My staff and recruits made me, and also broke me, as a head coach in big-time college athletics. It taught me a key lesson: do not hire or recruit a person who works for money, instead, seek those who will love the work or love the game.

ACQUIRING THE RIGHT PEOPLE

The most important thing we do as leaders is to surround ourselves with the right people. People are essential and they WILL either make or break you. Nothing, I will say it again, *nothing* is more important than the people you hire and recruit for your board, your leadership team, and your teammates.

It was never about me as the leader, the head coach. It was about hiring and recruiting the right people to make me better by shoring up my gaps and weaknesses. Unfortunately, hiring was the part of coaching I disliked the most. Leaders know exactly what I'm talking about. Our jobs and our successes depend on others and getting it right is very difficult. Each decision carries a burden of potential; the potential for success or failure. Certainty in hiring and recruiting is like a meteorologist's summer forecast—sometimes we get it exactly right, but more often small unknowns create a potential for clouds and rain.

Recruiting elite players, hiring talented assistant coaches, and selecting the best support staff for a major-college athletic team share common parallels with the business world's recruiting and hiring practices. Athletics may be a little different because we are selecting players who are between the ages of 15 to 18 and are still developing emotionally, intellectually, and physically. In collegiate basketball, with only three to four scholarships per year, we are afforded little to no opportunity for mistakes in our choices. It's like looking into a crystal ball to foresee their potential and to predict the impact of their unknown development on the team. Because my job performance and the team's ultimate success depended on 18- to 22-year-olds, an extra value was placed on the people I hired and chose to work with 14 to 16 hours a day, nearly 365 days a year.

MOTIVATING EACH INDIVIDUAL

After recruiting and hiring, the next challenge involves motivating each individual, keeping them engaged in the shared vision, and defining their roles and responsibilities. It is your job as an ON POINT leader to find out what motivates your people and team, individually and collectively.

The workplace consists of four generations today—Traditionalists, Baby Boomers, Generation Xers, and Millennials or Generation Y—and you can't manage or motivate each generation, or individual, the same way. If you are, you are probably frustrated, they are frustrated, and you are not getting the most out of your people and team. And, you are most likely struggling and probably failing as a leader in getting others to follow.

People stop me and often ask how I motivate people. After many years and experiences, I share the simple answer: *I ask them.* Sit down with your team and each individual and ask them what motivates them. Ask them how you can help them to perform at their best. Most of the time, leaders, managers, and coaches never ask. Effective coaches do this with their players, staff, and their teams at least four different times each year.

Does this sound like a quarterly performance review in the business world? Are you checking in with your team and people who need to be performing at their best, at the highest level? For me, the challenge was getting coaches and players to perform at the highest level individually, and as a team, in the public and in the national spotlight. They were performing on a national stage two to three times a week. This placed a lot of pressure, expectation, and stress on young people. The business world consists of adults and this should be easier for individuals who have a higher level of maturity, more life experience, and more resilience. Still, each business environment offers unique pressures and expectations that must be considered.

RETAINING TOP TALENT

Retaining top talent has every leader in every industry scratching their heads. Workplace turnover doesn't have a singular cause or solution. In our dynamic world, it's a societal challenge and it's showing up in every industry. For example, the transfer rate in college athletics is at an alarming rate and has skyrocketed every year. In 2014, college men's basketball had over 600 transfers. About 40 percent of all men's basketball players who play NCAA Division I basketball will transfer out of their initial school by the end of their sophomore year. College women's basketball had over 100 players transfer from major conference schools in 2015.

This is quite alarming for collegiate athletics, but corporate America experiences a similar, costly trend. According to a study by the Center for American Progress (CAP), the average cost to replace a staff member in today's workplace is 20 percent of an annual salary for mid-range positions (earning $30,000 to $50,000 a year). The cost to replace a $40,000 manager would be $8,000. For highly educated executive positions, CAP reports a replacement cost of *213 percent* of annual salary. The cost to replace a $200,000 CEO would be $426,000.

With millions of workers in the U.S. and an average turnover rate of 15.7 percent according to CompData Surveys, the lesson is as simple as the math is complicated. Coming up with a successful strategy to retain top talent is the multi-million (if not billion) dollar challenge. If leaders don't figure out how to hire, motivate, and retain staff, constant turnover will create unnecessary spending and render succession planning useless within the organization.

Internal promotion proved the value of succession planning in major-college football at the end of the 2015 season. Five big-time football programs, all from different conferences, promoted new head coaches from within their ranks. They all looked internally for the leader who would steer the ship and promoted coordinators to the head coaching positions. Although these organizations may not have predetermined this outcome, each of these scenarios represents the value of retaining staff, thoughtful succession planning, and long-term sustainability. They already had great people and talent inside the organization, and they were already preparing and training for this moment.

It's the same in business. This is a great strategy for organizations and provides stability, comfort, and sustainability for stakeholders, customers, the workforce and their families, and communities. This isn't to say that every organization will have their next CEO or leader in waiting, but organizations and teams should always take into account best practices to continue developing its people. It is an ON POINT leader's responsibility. If you do this, you will enable someone to step into a higher role, creating value for you and your team, as well as a healthy and long-lasting organization.

In business, retaining top talent can feel and seem impossible, even out of control. For today's workforce, the belief that moving on to the next best thing may be instilled as early as high school and perhaps middle school. Parents move their kids around to different youth teams, then different high schools, to maximize their child's opportunities. It's amazing how many kids have attended three or four high schools for those reasons. It spirals into college and eventually the workforce.

Our society, especially the Millennial generation, and fans, stakeholders, boards, trustees, the public, and media typically want instant gratification. This urgency paradigm influences the way we recruit and hire our team members. Historically we would bring people into our athletic programs and into our business organizations who want to be part of a larger purpose. Now we hear, *I want to be part of that, but am I going to be able to play as a freshman? When can I get a promotion? Will I have a six-figure salary? How fast can I move up the ladder in this company?* This is the way society is wired; people feel they haven't accomplished anything or have failed if their early careers don't have mercurial growth and continual rewards.

It's a vicious circle, and it's a condition that disappoints many organizations who put thousands (and millions) of dollars and resources into recruiting, hiring, and retaining talent for their organization. They can't figure out how to satisfy top talent and, consequently, the keys to retain them. This societal issue must be accepted as a "given" in today's world and it must be considered a top priority to resolve—sooner rather than later.

It's no wonder that it's harder to discipline children and teens today, in a culture of immediate gratification and constant recognition. And in business, it's harder for leaders and managers to provide constructive feedback, lay out expectations, and hold people accountable; employees have people from all sides telling them, *If you don't like it, or you don't like your boss, just leave.* The result is a culture of eroded loyalty and focus on "what have you done for me lately."

How many people in the financial industry take their "book" and go somewhere else because they don't want to follow the rules and they want to do things their way—instead of representing an organization that supported them for decades? In sports we would say they took their ball and went home. They didn't get to do things their way, someone held them accountable and asked them to behave differently, to change, and to follow the rules.

What can be done? It's our culture now and we created it, so we have to accept it and take action. For athletes, it started in youth sports, was reinforced in high school, and then became ingrained in college athletics. But this isn't just a sports problem; business leaders and organizations are dealing with this with grown adults, across all industries. (Are we having fun yet!?)

Ultimately, the solution is rather simple. Or at least it seems very simple, but becomes difficult because you have to find the right people and individuals for you and your team. Regardless of the up or down status of the economy, companies with the right people and the best talent, and the ability to motivate and to retain talent, are those that win. And, the discipline to do this over the long term represents the difference between fighting for survival and achieving sustainability.

If you want to retain talent, the greater your investment in professional development, mentoring, and coaching, the more likely you will keep the best of your best. This is critical within your organization because motivated people only want to get better and become the best. Those leaders who invest in their people are winning and will continue to win each and every year. They build a foundation for sustainable success, offer the best places to work, get the best talent, and create employees who do not want to leave.

The rules don't change if you're in major-college athletics or in business. In many ways, business leaders can relate to sports. (Although, regrettably, some sports clichés used in business should be retired, like "there's no 'I' in Team" or "give me 110 percent.") Sports is one of the best arenas to develop teams, leaders, teamwork, goals, work ethic, collaboration . . . and the list goes on and on. Whether our sports careers ended in grade school, high school, college, or the pros, we can all relate to lessons our coaches, teams, and wins and losses imparted.

RE-RECRUITING TALENT

I would like to share a final key element of this process that most people forget—or have never thought of—when it comes to retaining your best. If you want to keep your top talent and best people in order to establish stability, continuity, and eliminate as much turnover as possible, here is the secret sauce: *once you get them, you need to continue recruiting them.*

Here's the process I taught my team of recruiters and staff each year as we built our teams: Find Talent ⇨ Recruit ⇨ Build Relationships ⇨ Sign/Hire ⇨ Motivate ⇨ Continue Recruiting ⇨ Build Relationships ⇨ Develop. We scouted for talent, then recruited for the skills and cultural fit necessary for our program's success. With new players (and staff) in our sights, we built relationships based on trust, transparency, and mutual respect. We signed new players, hired new staff, and welcomed them to our program with a shared vision and values. Then we dedicated our time to motivating them—by understanding their unique needs and desires and customizing motivational approaches.

We continued re-recruiting our own players and staff through consistent messaging focused on the value they received from our program, and appreciating the contributions they made. We deepened our relationships, opening our hearts to share our fears and challenges, our hopes and dreams, our expectations and goals. To bring it all together, we developed individual and team skills, taking the natural talents players and staff brought to the program to new heights. Then, we repeated the cycle.

Can you apply this recipe for retention? If you emphasize continuous recruiting after you hire your team, build relationships, and routinely motivate and develop team members, you will most likely retain your best people and top talent. If you think the most important objective of your job is to produce results, don't kid yourself—you can't guarantee long-term performance success if you spend most of your time replacing and retraining team members and troubleshooting team problems. Build and develop your team the right way and results will follow.

Follow these four principles for recruiting and retaining top talent:

1. *Hire the right people who fit your values; do not sacrifice your values.* Communicate your values, expectations, and vision before bringing new contributors into your organization. Many times, it's the employer's fault for making the wrong hire or not recruiting the right fit. If your organization

suffks from poor retention rates, it's probably because you're not exe-cuting thorough hiring practices to get to the right person.

2.   *Surround yourself with people brighter than you and who will challenge you to be better.* To do this, you need to be secure in your own abilities and believe in yourself. It's not about you; it's about the talent that surrounds you. This is a must in order to experience success and to be the best. Many leaders are too insecure to hire people better and smarter than they are. Insecure leaders surround themselves with "YES" people.

3.   *Favor people who are dedicated, demonstrate work ethic, and have great potential—over pure talent.* Identify knowledge, tendencies, strengths, and skillsets needed on the team. Are you creating a new position or filling one? Leaders often lose their jobs because they hire the wrong people. Hire people who want to be part of your organization. This is extremely valuable and, most of the time, even more important than someone with greater skill. It's easier to develop and coach skills than to create some-one's attitude.

4.   *After you recruit or hire your team members, you must continue recruiting them.* This is the single most important aspect that most leaders forget—or have never considered. Use these proven best practices to keep your best: listen to them, engage their hearts and minds, include them on proj-ects, be collaborative, hold them accountable, provide instant feedback, allow flexibility, value their contributions, provide coaching and training, and create a healthy culture.

On April 16, 2015, I attended the 2015 WNBA Draft. Top talent was all around me—the best of the best skillsets and emerging leaders. I had 12 professional athletes surrounding me for several days leading up to the draft and, as the pres-ident of the league announced the names, dreams came true. One of my former players was drafted second overall. It was a great moment for her and for me, as a proud coach and second mom. It was energizing being around individuals with top talent, both physical and mental. The way they think, speak, and carry themselves is unique. The 2015 draft was the third I'd attended in the past 10 years. It was a poignant and pointed reminder as a coach and consultant of the principles of good recruiting, development, and retention of top talent in leading organizations.

Retention of top talent is one of the hottest topics in corporate America and college athletics. Is it the Millennial generation or are organizations falling short in their hiring and recruiting strategies? Is it a lack of professional development opportunities for employees? Have company leadership teams progressed or are they leading the same way they did 10 years ago? Who is taking responsibility for employee tenure?

Here's the deal: Millennials are the largest generation currently in the workforce. The U.S. labor force is bimodal with lots of older workers, lots of younger ones, and fewer people in the middle. This presents a significant managerial challenge that relates to the rise and fall of the talent economy. We work within a much more service-based environment, with intellectual property being key, compared to 50 years ago when we operated in a manufacturing, durable-goods economy. I believe management has not kept up with this change in the workforce.

My experience in working with leading companies is this: unsuccessful companies are not providing the flexibility, professional development, feedback, leadership, and growth opportunities that a modern worker needs in order to thrive and to stay competitive. As the economy improves, job-hopping will increase because a better economy equals more opportunity.

Let's talk about Millennials more. Here are my thoughts for you, the Baby Boomer executive, and you, the Gen X senior leader. Understand that Millennials are not the first generation to be called lazy. This popular perception was similar for Gen Xers and even for Baby Boomers. Remember the refrain from the 60s? *Cut your hair, get a job!* My advice to you: get over it and embrace them. A Millennial will be your boss someday, if not today.

More than 90 percent of Millennials expect to stay in a job for less than three years, according to the 2012 Future Workplace "Multiple Generations @ Work" survey of 1,189 employees and 150 managers. What can you do to change this?

Embrace this generation; if you don't, you don't get it and you and your organization will lose. If you find yourself frustrated managing Millennials, you are part of the problem. Once you realize you will learn from their unique skillset, and develop the competencies you need to collaborate with them, you will grow and stay relevant.

The number one request for Millennials is for consistent and immediate feedback. Good or bad, they want feedback now, not the traditional once-a-year review. I must say, I agree with this. How can you improve, develop, and be held accountable when you only receive a traditional once-a-year evaluation? This is an unreasonable, and unsustainable, expectation that owes its existence to habit and "the way we've always done it." In fact, progressive organizations today, like Netflix, Accenture, and even GE are eliminating the traditional annual performance evaluation.

Debbie was my client for a year. She was a very successful and established Executive Vice President who had been with the same organization for more than 20 years. She hired me because she wanted to reach the next level as a leader, she wanted to get better, and she wanted feedback. She had not experienced a performance evaluation, received constructive feedback, or had someone who held her accountable for more than 20 years.

What? How does this happen?

As a competitive and driven executive, wouldn't you want to know how you can improve and be the best in your industry? Debbie did. Over the course of our coaching engagement, I gathered and provided her with the feedback she was looking for from her bosses, peers, direct reports, and clients. This feedback changed her professional life, her career trajectory, and the experience of others working with her.

How in the world can today's leaders not clarify expectations, provide feedback, and engender accountability with their people and teams? Debbie did not leave the organization, as she wants to continue working for another 15 years. But for goodness sake, a leader job must at least fulfill this need. You owe this to the people who work for you and the company's stakeholders who expect performance to improve.

So if you see a lot of turnover in your organization, most likely it's the employer's fault. And who represents the daily proxy for the employer? The leaders. Take a look in the mirror.

AVOIDING "YES" PEOPLE

We all learn from mistakes. Most of my mistakes occurred mid-career, when I inadvertently hired a bunch of "yes" people. They were hesitant to share their ideas, opinions, and thoughts. They were intimidated or easily afraid. We were stagnant and I wasn't getting what I wanted and needed from my staff and people who I expected to make me better.

Clearly, this did not help me as a leader. I didn't feel I had enough help and, as a result, our program and organization struggled. It wasn't enough that they were aligned with our vision, values, and goals. The problem was that as a leader I needed people around me who were going to challenge me and make me better. And, for our program to succeed, we all needed such an environment.

I did not have "yes" people on my staff at the beginning and the end of my coaching tenure. What I had were the right people with a variety of skills and talent who made the organization and me better as a head coach and leader. We were not afraid to challenge each other. We didn't always agree but we were always professional and we respected and understood the process—trust and challenge each other, hold each other accountable, and handle conflict in a healthy manner. The years when I had a staff that challenged me proved to be my best years.

As a leader, you need to strike the right balance between providing direction and welcoming input. Don't be afraid to let others challenge your ideas, thoughts, and decisions. Ask people in your organization to speak up, give feedback, and hold you accountable. A great tool I've found is to bust out of your network. Go outside of your own walls and industry; use an external trusted advisor or a personal coach. They won't feel constrained by the boss-subordinate relationship or worried about their jobs—they will tell you what you must hear, like it or not.

To retain top talent, you have got to be the real deal. An ON POINT leader welcomes challenges from others and thrives in the up, down, and lateral discussions that need to occur in real-time for your business to thrive—in this era and beyond.

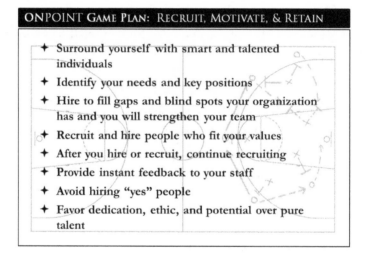

ONPOINT GAME PLAN: RECRUIT, MOTIVATE, & RETAIN

+ Surround yourself with smart and talented individuals
+ Identify your needs and key positions
+ Hire to fill gaps and blind spots your organization has and you will strengthen your team
+ Recruit and hire people who fit your values
+ After you hire or recruit, continue recruiting
+ Provide instant feedback to your staff
+ Avoid hiring "yes" people
+ Favor dedication, ethic, and potential over pure talent

BUILDING HIGH-PERFORMING TEAMS

"Alone we can do so little, together we can do so much."
–Helen Keller–

Building teams is easy to talk about but many leaders don't know where to start or the first thing about how to do it successfully. To add to the challenge of composing a team, the focus quickly shifts to building high-performing teams, consistently, over and over. There are very few leaders in business or athletics who have the formula or leadership acumen to accomplish this year after year.

Every year we held our first team meeting on the first day of classes. The room was loud and vibrant, and filled with laughter and many hugs. It was great to see everyone back on campus and ready to go for another exciting year. As the 2003-2004 season began, our team had just come off the best season in program history: 25 wins and a Sweet 16 appearance, with the added distinction of breaking Stanford's 27-game home winning streak (more than two-and-a-half years of not losing a game at home). We were building on a fun, great season and were excited to kick off a new year.

I started the team meeting off by welcoming everyone back. I had an agenda in front of me with many topics and various logistics to cover

over the next hour. As I completed the first part of my agenda, one of my top returning players and captains raised her hand. I looked at her and said, *Can you wait just a couple more minutes before I answer any questions?* She put her hand down and started fidgeting. Two minutes later she raised her hand again, and I looked at her and said, *I'm almost finished.* She put her hand down again. A minute later she raised her hand for the third time. This time, I responded, *Ok, what do you have to say?*

She said, *Coach . . . I know we went to the Sweet 16 last year, but this year I want to go to the Final Four.* As her statement floated around the room and settled in, I felt like my jaw hit the floor and time froze. I was actually jumping up and down inside and so fired up I could scream. Very calmly I looked at her and said, *You want to go to the Final Four? So do I!* I looked around the room at the rest of the team and they were smiling ear to ear and wringing their hands together. The freshman looked like they'd seen a ghost.

Exactly eight months later, we were playing in the program's first-ever Final Four in New Orleans. During the journey to the Final Four, teamwork was many acting as ONE. We were selfless. It was all about the process and the journey of building this special and high-performing team—just getting a little bit better each day.

FROM MANY TO ONE

The key to build a high-performing team is to focus on the strengths of individuals and what they do well. This may seem obvious, yet many leaders, coaches, and managers often put all the focus on what people and their teams can't do. Most of us have been around people like this—their thinking, planning, and conversations are all about what their people and teams can't do and what they're not good at. They spend all their time plugging holes and filling gaps instead of building on existing capabilities. Leveraging strengths creates a mindset of winning, reinforces positivity, and paves the path to reach peak performance.

I have built and assembled many winning teams in 27 years of coaching college basketball. As a senior executive coach, I now specialize in building high-performing and highly functional teams in business. In working in business and coaching teams, we focus on building winning teams and enabling growth. My responsibility as a coach in business is to hold my clients accountable to take the necessary steps in building a high-performing, functional team that is growing and successful. In building a winning team, place your focus and emphasis on these seven attributes as a team's strong foundation:

1. Create an inspiring shared vision

2. Establish roles and responsibilities

3. Set goals and expectations

4. Develop strategies to accomplish your goals

5. Communicate and address conflicts

6. Execute the plan

7. Cultivate a culture of accountability

In 2004, beating Duke to reach the Final Four was one of the highlights of my University of Minnesota coaching career. Our vision for accomplishing this goal was discussed in our first team meeting at the beginning of the year. From the time it escaped my team captain's mouth, this was our team's vision from day one.

This team was a high-performing and well-oiled machine. Everything that led up to the Final Four was surreal. Over the course of the year, we built a winning team in every aspect. We set short and long-term goals as a team and celebrated small successes together. The year and season are long and daunting so we set early-season, mid-season, regular-season, and post-season goals. In business, you can relate this to monthly, quarterly, and annual goals. We set goals and expectations as an entire team and this created buy-in, collaboration, and ownership. I have worked with leaders who tell their employees what their goals are for the year. This directive approach does not work; involve your people and you will see your people invest more in their goals.

After setting goals with your team, you must determine your strategy. What is your game plan and strategy to accomplish these goals? Recently, working with one of my teams in the business world, they presented me their team's goals for the coming year. They were very thoughtful, organized, challenging, and specific. I said, *Great job!* Then I challenged them with the next step and asked, *How do you plan on reaching these goals? What is your strategy and game plan to accomplish your goals?* The entire team froze. They looked at me and said, *I guess we have more work to do.* It's great to set goals, but break it down so you know how you are going to get there.

I mentioned early in this chapter that the key to building high-performing teams is to identify individuals' strengths. Identifying roles and responsibilities on your team and in your organization is empowering to everyone on the team. It's fun, it's energizing, and it allows everyone to operate at a high level and to do what they do best. No one does this better than elite coaches and athletes. Players know who is supposed to take the shot, be the team's leading rebounder, be the defensive stopper, set the screen, or run the offense from the point. In business, we often face a struggle because many team members want to be the star and they don't understand that the role players will make or break every team. Make sure everyone's roles and responsibilities are clear, that everyone understands what they are, and that there is ultimate buy-in.

Clear and concise goals and expectations should be communicated to each individual and the team. There should be no doubt or gray area about the expectations, roles and responsibilities, and the execution of the plan from each team member. In athletics, business, and life, communication is not only one of the key contributors to success, it is also the one that breaks down and derails every team. Conflict avoidance, miscommunication, and unclear expectations will lead to problems that cause teams to unravel. How a team communicates and addresses conflicts within the team should also be discussed. This is a key component for feedback and accountability.

The final attribute is to cultivate a culture of accountability. What is accountability? Accountability is my complete acknowledgement of, and acceptance of, the effects of my behaviors and actions. Accountability is the alignment of what I say I'll do and what I actually do. Put another way, accountability is fulfilling my commitment to my team and myself. Being able to hold yourself accountable is first and foremost. Are you doing what you said you were going to do? Second, you need to have accountability within your team. Do you have strong leaders *within* your team, organization, and business who hold each other accountable? Then, as a leader, are you holding yourself and the people around you accountable? Don't let yourself or your team off the hook.

WE GOT YOU, COACH

Many leaders and many teams lack accountability. Most leaders fall short through their inability to handle conflict, have hard conversations, and hold people to what is expected. As a basketball and executive coach, I have helped leaders hold themselves accountable by helping them become more self-aware. I have held them accountable for having hard conversations with their staff and for implementing hard deadlines for projects. I have required them to hold staff meetings to support communication, clarify expectations, develop leaders, and reinforce accountability. It's amazing how many businesses and team leaders do not have team meetings (except when something goes wrong). This creates bad communications habits, allows staff to "write their own stories" about expectations, and typically results in a breakdown in accountability and damage to the bottom line.

Our first game in the NCAA Tournament on our run to the Final Four was against UCLA. They were a tough opponent and we did not match up well with their team. Their strengths were our weaknesses. However, we won the game 92-81 in front of a home crowd of 12,357 passionate fans. We advanced to the second round and took on the number two seed Kansas State in front of a raucous crowd of 13,425 fans in the loudest arena I had ever experienced. The basket was as big as the ocean and our defense was firing on all cylinders. We blew out the Wildcats 80-61 to advance to the Sweet 16.

We travelled to Norfolk, Virginia, to play third-seeded Boston College in the Sweet 16. It was a bittersweet matchup; before arriving at the University of Minnesota, I was the associate head coach at Boston College. I had recruited every player on that team and I was coaching against people who I loved dearly. I knew that winning this game would end their season, finish some of their playing careers, and break their hearts. I never experienced greater internal conflict, emotion, and duress before any game I played or coached. We beat Boston College 76-63 and advanced to the Elite Eight for the first time in school history to take on the number-one seeded Duke Blue Devils. Now, this team, our program, and my players had reached the biggest test they'd ever faced.

I had two very special players on my team and in my corner. These two players together were a significant force. They were leaders that any coach and business would love to have on their team. They bought into our vision and before games of this magnitude they would say, *We got you coach, we got this, we'll take care of this.* They would slap my back, head out to the floor, and take care of business. For a coach and leader, this was reassuring and brought me so much confidence.

How did we get to *We got you coach?* My team knew I loved them like they were my own daughters. There was mutual respect and loyalty, and they knew I had their back on and off the court, as players and as people. We provided the vision, a healthy culture, and a system that allowed people and the team to flourish. They were coachable and we provided a nurturing environment where team members felt safe. Together, we trusted each other and would do anything for each other's success.

Duke, on the other hand, made a critical mistake: they looked past us. Their team had already made dinner plans to celebrate a win and booked travel arrangements for the Final Four. When I heard this, I shared it with my captains and leaders. I knew they were competitive and would influence the other players. I remember giving them the newspaper with the article and saying, *Read this.* They read it. Then they smiled and said, *We got this coach, we will take care of this.*

Before the game we had an emotional pre-game meeting at the hotel. We asked each player to reflect on the season and to write down what it would mean to them to win this game and to achieve our program's first Final Four. Everyone shared what they wrote and the emotions in that room created a powerful team dynamic. We left the room confident and our players had that focused, unyielding look in their eyes: I knew at that moment we would win this game.

Duke arrived at our matchup after a 27-3 regular season, earning a number one tournament seed. We were an at-large qualifying team with a regular season record of 21-8 and held a seventh seed. It's extremely rare for a seventh seed in women's college basketball to make it to the Final Four. But, 40 minutes later the final buzzer sounded and we had won 82-75. We'd made history again for the Minnesota program.

More importantly, we believed. We believed in each other, in the process, and in ourselves. We had a vision and stated expectations to get to the Final Four. Roles were clearly defined and communicated, and the players bought into them. The team and staff performed to our potential and we were on our way to the Final Four.

We faced a 30-win Connecticut Huskies juggernaut in the Final Four. Frankly, no one was getting past the Huskies that year. Indeed, they beat us 67-58 in a competitive game in front of 18,211 fans, then went on to win the national championship. Despite the loss, we built a winning team and had a magical year! Sharing a compelling vision, having high expectations, setting goals and a strategy to achieve them, then executing and holding each other accountable was a recipe for success.

Building highly functional and high-performing teams is easy to talk about but many leaders don't know where to start. Achieving this year after year is the goal, and there are many factors that will influence your success. An ON POINT leader will strive to build a winning team through a game plan that converts an inspiring vision into clear goals, roles, and expectations for their team. When that team hits the floor, anything is possible.

ONPOINT GAME PLAN: BUILD HIGH-PERFORMING TEAMS

✦ Create an inspiring vision for your team and organization

✦ Establish roles and responsibilities and ensure that everyone accepts their role

✦ Set goals and expectations for each individual and the team

✦ Develop strategies to accomplish your goals

✦ Emphasize communication and address conflicts

✦ Execute the plan

✦ Create a culture of accountability

CREATING CHAMPIONS

"Champions aren't made in gyms. Champions are made from something they have deep inside them—a desire, a dream, a vision. They have to have the skill. And the will. But the will must be stronger than the skill. "
–Muhammed Ali–

When your third-string quarterback comes off the bench magnificently, your walk-on forward earns a starting position and hits a buzzer-beating shot to win the game, or your executive assistant progresses to become your indispensable chief of staff, there's one common denominator: a championship culture. Such a culture is one in which every individual is important, every contribution is valued, and every individual elevates the team over his or her own success. The strength of the culture keeps jealousy and other harmful behaviors at bay, and lifts all team members to performance heights above and beyond the norm.

CHAMPIONSHIP CULTURE

In athletics, players are taught and trained to execute a 12-month, season-long program; in business, the expectations should be the same. The overriding objective is to engage the team in something that's greater than the individual and to ensure everyone understands and experiences that calling. This condition—essential to high performance—creates a championship culture that mints champions.

Few executive leaders understand how to architect a culture that creates and supports champions. Are you one of them? Successful coaches and leaders cultivate and nurture a culture that hinges on a selfless, team-first philosophy and approach. How are the individuals ready to perform when their number is called? Will they step right onto the playing field and execute at a high level? Will the other team members support their success? Will the team function without missing a beat?

The ON POINT leader creates a championship culture; your head coach, position coach, manager, supervisor, director, vice president, CEO, and team understand and serve a greater purpose. As an athletic or executive coach, you wish you could just bottle it, because at times it is so strong and powerful, almost other-worldly and magical. When you experience it, anything is possible, from the biggest comeback or most unlikely upset to the most dominating victory. These moments, these conditions of excellence, forge champions throughout the team or organization. Every leader in every industry strives to achieve a vision and to create a collaborative championship team culture like this.

In most organizations and teams, very few understand what it takes to build a championship culture. According to Jeff Janssen in *Championship Team Building*, effective teams spend a majority of their energy externally, focusing on and working toward their common goal. They devote 90 percent of their time and energy productively pursuing their goals. Moderately effective teams spend 50 percent of their time focused on their goals and the other half trying to overcome internal problems. Ineffective teams spend the majority of their time, 90 percent, dealing with internal problems and conflict, which leaves a fraction of time left to focus on their goals. These leaders, teams, and organizations don't make it. ON POINT leaders know how to create champions and will break down walls to achieve a culture many will never experience. Simple flaws lead to negative perceptions from those around you and subvert the culture you desire. A subtle expression of belief and support for your people will make all the difference in your journey to the top.

Once you've reached that rarified air at the top, the ability to handle success is a common problem, often because the focus on previous accomplishments enables complacency that prevents continuous growth and even loftier success. And, high achievers and top producers often resist change in their approaches to interpersonal relationships. However, what worked in the past doesn't necessarily work today. The world evolves and changes every day. The good news is, one's approach can be tweaked which is necessary to create a championship culture and champions.

CHAMPIONSHIP BEHAVIOR

Organizational cultures are organic: they grow and evolve over time and take new shapes and forms depending on environmental conditions. How can you intentionally design a culture? If it was so easy, wouldn't everyone do it? It's not easy, but it's not magical or mystical either. To create the culture you want, you must identify, model, recognize and reward, and repeat the behaviors and actions you want the culture to embody. Remove the mystique and reverence with which we discuss culture; it's simply about putting in the work to emphasize the characteristics and the values you choose.

Over and over and over, the intentional designer of culture relentlessly reinforces desired cultural behaviors and actions. You fill the organization's space by nurturing chosen activities, leaving little to no space for an undesirable culture to take root and to flourish. The leader's role is pivotal in designing and reinforcing a championship culture. Leader behaviors and actions radiate out, influencing those around them and sowing the seeds of organizational culture.

Here are 10 leader-focused elements to build a championship culture foundation:

1. *Identify your strengths.* When was the last time you focused on yourself? What are your strengths? Do what you do and do it better than anyone else. Leverage your strengths to benefit the team.

2. *Align and lead with your values.* Your personal and professional values should be aligned. Your values at home should be intertwined with those at work. This is a big reason many women leave their jobs. And today, more men are experiencing work-life imbalances. Leading with your val-

ues means leading confidently in the direction of what is important to you and what you and your organization stand for.

3. *Listen.* Listening is one of the most important leadership skills to develop. This is on every client's goal sheet. Those around you want to be heard. We say we care and want certain things from our players, our employees, our team; listening is the doorway to demonstrate caring and to encourage contribution. Hone your listening skills.

4. *Delegate.* Get out of the weeds and stop micromanaging. This is a very hard skill to learn, but when you do, it's amazing. Giving up what you think defines "control" enables champions to develop around you. Trust and have confidence in your people and team. Instead of doing it all yourself, spend your time coaching performance, removing barriers, and encouraging your team members.

5. *Develop people.* To reach upper levels of leadership, a leader must transition from a producer to a developer. There is nothing more important than coaching your people and teams. A single producer creates value reliably, but multiple producers create value exponentially.

6. *Show vulnerability.* Vulnerability takes a high level of courage and confidence. When a leader gets comfortable with who they are, when they feel secure and are human around their teams, barriers and walls crumble all around the team. All my players ever wanted was to see that I was human and that I cried, laughed, smiled, and admitted to my mistakes. One of my players was shocked when she found out that I ate potato chips. The people around you want to understand and to relate to you.

7. *Practice effective communication.* Many challenges and issues are created by ineffective communication. Strong, effective leaders stress fundamentals, discipline, expectations, accountability, and buy-in. You will get exactly what you expect as a leader, so be clear and persistent in your messaging.

8. *Set and maintain expectations.* Top leaders will always maintain high expectations. They will communicate their expectations clearly and promote high standards. Your goals should be treated as expectations. If they aren't, why set them in the first place?

9. *Enable buy-in.* Deliver an inspiring vision to align individual and team expectations and actions. Everyone has different roles and responsibilities; when every team member accepts and performs to their role, then supports each other, a championship culture grows.

10. *Ensure accountability.* Why are leaders afraid to hold people and teams accountable? People want it and will respect you for it. This is a critical role and skill for an ON POINT leader. Holding people accountable will advance high quality and deliver championship results.

> " In order to control your **DESTINY**, take control of your repetitive **BEHAVIORS**. One of the masters of executive coaching, Tony Robbins, says it best: *It's not what we do once in a while that shapes our lives, but what we do* **CONSISTENTLY.** "

My high school coach had a basic equation to pave the path for creating champions: practice harder, work smarter, and make adjustments along the way. It's about preparation, routines, and agility to situational change. Muhammed Ali often discussed his training with contempt. He didn't like to train, but he imposed his will to continue under the pretense that if he suffered now, he would live the rest of his life as a champion. He was right. First, learn to become your own champion and then it will be easier to create other champions around you.

NEXT-LEVEL PERFORMANCE

Clients engage coaches to assist them with their journey as leaders, managing people, leading teams, and balancing their own personal lives. Often, it's the highest achievers who are competitive, played sports, or have children who are playing competitive sports. These leaders recognize that transferable skills and lessons from athletics may be applied effectively to the machine of business and to the complexities of our own personal and professional lives.

It's a challenge for someone who's a high achiever to take it to a championship level. I work with many people and teams who are already very successful and at the top of their game. Complacency poses threats to future success. How then do we create champions?

For senior-level leaders, becoming a champion involves improving their leadership skills and effectiveness just incrementally, *about five to seven percent*. We assume high-level leaders already operate at 85 percent of their capability—it's not a coincidence the senior leader sits in that chair, there's a reason. The diverse experiences we all face change how we lead or coach. Health issues, family crisis, losing a job, firing an employee, and many other conditions can change how we lead dramatically.

Experiencing a certain level of success raises the pressure and expectation of future performance. In my experience, most leaders aren't really prepared for that level of success and, at times, the ensuing requirements knock you back on your heels. We start feeling aches and pains in all parts of our minds and bodies; we respond by thinking we are Superman or Wonder Woman and we try to plow through everything. When you experience this and you re-evaluate, an executive coach can help you explore and execute new ways to improve and to run your organization.

Convince yourself that things need to change. Creating champions starts with yourself and learning how to be agile when you're facing change. People are motivated differently; they have different strengths and styles and are unique. We're not all made the same, nor are we equal in our talents and capabilities, and we all bring different baggage to the organization—much of which has nothing to do with work.

It's our job as ON POINT leaders to determine how to get the best out of individuals and our teams. You will have a mix of resources on a project or team, from the best and most expert staff members to those with less experience and capabilities, and it's the leader's responsibility to create champions in everyone. Those individuals exhibit great talents and when a leader can combine the talents by enabling the team to work together, something special occurs: a force multiplier for team performance and results!

It's incredibly powerful when it all comes together. It's a great feeling when a team collaborates, shares ideas, challenges each other, builds trust, celebrates successes, and has fun. As coaches and leaders, we may think we are doing someone a favor if we can just win another game or we can reach numbers that quarter. But if we don't take care of ourselves as leaders and value people around us, none of that matters.

Leaders who strive to get to the next level and create champions need to embrace delegation and stop micromanaging. You are very fortunate if you've experienced so much success that you've created a monster. But, when you create a monster you have to feed it. As a leader, lock up that do-it-all monster and focus on creating champions and building a championship culture day in and day out. It may be difficult to shut the monster down and stop. Again, you need to learn to become a champion yourself. Hit the gym or exercise to stay physically healthy, understand your "why" to keep mentally healthy, and invest time in learning how to involve and to engage your team members.

Throughout my coaching career in athletics and business I have focused on creating and building champions in life. A major element involves instilling confidence in my players and now in my clients and the individuals who work in their organizations. I learned to surround myself with people who want more and who are not satisfied with the status quo. I sought clients who are top performers and producers and who want to be pushed to be respected leaders. They are leaders who want to become champions and who are committed to developing a championship culture. Most importantly, they are willing to change their leadership styles and behaviors in order to get there.

Start by asking yourself if you really want to be ON POINT and if you are willing to accept the responsibility in creating a championship culture. First, pick a few critical traits that you want to improve and start there. Have confidence in yourself and, most importantly, instill it in those around you. Value everyone from the janitor to the CEO. Throw out considerations of role, title, salary, from the front lines to the back office—a championship culture means valuing every single individual equally for their unique talents and abilities to contribute. *People matter.*

Have courage to enter the abyss where many leaders and organizations fear to tread. That is where ON POINT leaders make their living and make a difference. Yes, there will be days when you fall, make mistakes, get bruised, and earn floor burns. My friends, in those falls you will find the gold from which championship cultures are molded.

ON POINT GAME PLAN: CREATE CHAMPIONS

+ Intentionally design your culture
+ Align and lead with your values
+ Listen actively and demonstrate care
+ Delegate and involve others
+ Develop people
+ Show vulnerability
+ Practice effective communication
+ Set and maintain expectations
+ Enable buy-in and ensure accountability
+ Take it to the next level of performance

A DRIVEN AND
CARING LEADER

*"We delight in the beauty of the butterfly, but rarely admit the
changes it has gone through to achieve that beauty."*
—Maya Angelou—

**For coaches to get the most out of their elite players and teams, we
have to "coach'em up."** Have you heard that before?

Great leaders and coaches coach'em up! They get the most out of their
teams and people by being driven and caring leaders. Leaders don't worry
about what's best for them, but instead focus on others' needs and on
developing people into more than they could ever imagine.

It's a great honor to be in a position of leadership, to share a clear vision
with those you are leading, and to take your team to a place better than
they thought they were capable of going. Not only is it an honor, it is an
obligation of the ON POINT leader.

Situations are best if you treat everyone in your workplace and team as
a member of your family. Why? *Because they are.* With all the complexities
of any team, the structure is just like family. You have the opportunity to
inspire, listen, empower, and provide honest feedback. Through these actions, you can cultivate the best performance from the team. Healthy teams
see feedback as an opportunity to build people up, not tear them down.

THE GIFT OF FEEDBACK

One of the greatest gifts a leader can give is honest feedback. Have you heard the saying, *No news is good news?* Well, that's false. Leaders, managers, and coaches should provide feedback on a consistent basis. It's a disservice to members of your team not to share your knowledge and spread enthusiasm when people do things right.

Would you like your boss to tell you what you want to hear rather than tell you what you need to hear? I have coached many elite athletes who are hungry for feedback. They were all pleasers and didn't want to disappoint me. They didn't want to let me down. Athletes want feedback and input on areas to improve, just like those of us in the workforce. It's no different.

As a senior executive coach, my clients are starving for feedback. I work with successful leaders who have been in senior-level leadership positions for decades. They're in these positions for a reason: they are highly skilled, knowledgeable, and successful at what they do. And the really good leaders want that feedback. They recognize how important a two-way dialogue is with their team.

Professionals are working longer hours. They are also working more efficiently and retiring later. Imagine how much more potent they would be if they received constant feedback on their strengths and opportunities for growth? Consider this: the successful ones wouldn't be successful if they weren't curious and life-long learners. They are craving opportunities to improve! You should never be too proud or too sure of yourself to ask for feedback. And, you should never be too busy to help your team grow professionally.

Early in my coaching career, this was a shortfall of mine. As a young basketball coach, I didn't provide feedback as much as I should have. I ignored the bottom of our ranks. I primarily coached all of those on the top and in the middle. What a shame! Our struggling players were craving my knowledge so they could improve. Lack of feedback kept them from reaching their full potential, and even more importantly, these players didn't get much playing time or attention. They deserved my coaching as much as anyone on the team, but I wasn't as forthcoming with feedback or aggressively coaching them as I should have been.

What I learned was to focus on coaching everyone up. My teams were optimized when I was able to get each player and staff member to see and to believe how uniquely special they were and to provide them with specific feedback to help them grow. I discovered that even if they weren't the most talented, if I could inspire and influence them by focusing on their strengths and delivering the motivation they thirsted for, greatness would result. If I failed to attend to every team member, the fabric of the team would threaten to unravel.

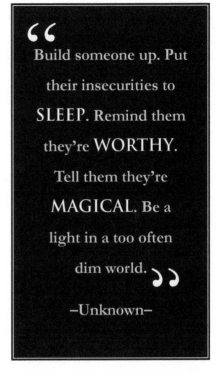

" Build someone up. Put their insecurities to SLEEP. Remind them they're WORTHY. Tell them they're MAGICAL. Be a light in a too often dim world. "

–Unknown–

My players were student-athletes; as a driven and caring coach, it was my duty to coach'em up *on and off* the court. I made them believe and gave them the courage to face a very difficult academic test or personal challenge off the court. On the court each day, my role as a driven and caring coach was to get the best out of each one of the players, to help them perform at their highest level. The ability to coach people up required me to provide encouragement, reinforce positivity, and communicate their value.

While building relationships, each team member needed to know that I cared about them. This was the ingredient that I needed as a leader and coach to drive them and to push them to a level not even they thought they could reach. How many examples do we see today, in sports and business, of coaches and leaders intimidating and disparaging their team members, rather than caring for and building them up? Unfortunately, it's everywhere.

Building genuine relationships with my team members as people allowed me as a leader to push, coach, challenge, and, at times, give them the kick in the butt they needed. As a leader, I would sacrifice some talent in order to get the attributes on my team that couldn't be coached: a good attitude and a strong work ethic. Coaching up requires acquiring people with the right values and characteristics, then being a driven and caring leader—that's your job as a leader of any team and organization. A coach's and leader's responsibility is to make your people and teams believe they can do more than they think they can. A special leader is one others want to follow and makes people believe they can do more than what's possible. Great leaders know how to push people and teams beyond comfortable, habitual boundaries.

This is a leader's responsibility! A driven, caring leader is authentic and will get the best results. Your people will run through a wall for you, they will go to and beyond their limits, they will do whatever it takes, they won't let you down, and they will give you their best effort each and every day.

THE VALUE OF OPTIMISM

How would you rate your ability as a leader to share an inspiring vision, get buy-in from everyone on your team, acknowledge strengths, collaborate openly, and allow innovation and creativity with your people and within your organization?

As an effective leader and coach, it's critical to leverage the power of positivity through your actions and words. As a basketball coach, learning how to motivate people to achieve results required me to develop people, and having a positive impact in their development was a huge responsibility and one of the most rewarding I ever experienced. Now, as a coach in business, I experience that reward daily with my clients. To be able to positively impact and enrich lives personally and professionally, as leaders and with their teams, is the best experience a coach can have.

Each year required a different strategy to coach up my players and teams. Each team and its challenges were unique each year. Do you coach and lead the same way each day, each year, and in good as well as bad times? If so, you might not realize the true potential that lives within each team.

I learned through many years of experience, through trial and error, until I found my ideal formula for how to be a driven, competitive, caring coach and leader. I learned how to get the best out of each individual and team. To drive my teams and players, I would push harder, challenge them more, care about them more deeply, and provide more constructive feedback. Every coach provides feedback after a loss (and sometimes players even listen), but I began to provide specific feedback after wins. They could take it. Coming off a big win (of course, *all* wins were big), which is a big rush for a player and coach to experience, their confidence was already sky-high. They thrived, they were confident, and they knew we were not settling, but had to continue to improve.

After losses, guess what? As a driven, competitive, caring coach and leader, after a loss I learned that I needed to employ a different feedback approach to get the best out of each individual and the team. My players and staff were natural pleasers; they didn't ever want to let me down, they wanted to perform well and win for their coach, and they truly tried not to make mistakes or lose. I bet you have the same type of people around you. Coming down hard on my staff and players after a loss wasn't the right approach; they were already more upset about losing and with themselves than I ever could have been. Being positive and constructive, giving high fives and smiles, and emphasizing hard work turned out to be the most effective approach to prepare them for the next Big Ten battle later that week. Building them up as people and athletes instead of tearing them down proved to be the best approach for long-term success.

Athletics is the same as business. Are you a driven and caring leader only when things are going well? The people around you need you to lead with this approach when things are not going well more than ever. It's easy to lead when things are going well. Anyone can lead when conditions are positive and you're winning. But your true colors come out as a leader when things are not going well, when you're losing and under fire.

In 2004, my team was playing at Northwestern University, which was always a difficult place to play. Playing on the road in the Big Ten was brutal and if you could win half of your road games each year and take care of business at home, you would be in great shape to contend for the Big Ten championship and to earn a berth to the NCAA Tournament. This particular night wasn't going our way for the game's first 32 minutes. It was one of the ugliest games I have ever seen. With eight minutes remaining in the game, we were down 16 points and falling fast.

I tried Plan A, Plan B, and Plan C and nothing seemed to work. I had a senior on the bench who was a great person and teammate; she was hard working but not the most talented player. I believed in her so I put her in the game, looking to spark the team. As she got up from the bench and walked over to report into the game, I smiled and put my arm around her, said a few words of encouragement, and told her to play hard, make the most of the opportunity, and play the last eight minutes to win the game. For those eight minutes, we used every full- and half-court press in our playbook. We put pressure on Northwestern, caused turnovers, and erased the deficit. Miraculously, we came back and won the game—and a senior off the bench who rarely played sparked the victory and was the player of the game. As a veteran and senior player, there was no way she was going to let our team lose this game.

Believing in people and coaching them up to perform, even in seemingly impossible circumstances, happened this night on the road in the Big Ten. It was a great lesson to me and to my team: any player or team member, when given the opportunity and support to succeed, can drive the team to victory.

THE LEADER'S IDENTITY

An athletic team always takes on the identity of the coach. In business, your organization and team will always take on the identity of their team leader. What is the identity of your team? Do you like what you see? If you do, they have taken on your identity as a leader. If you don't, they have taken on your identity as a leader.

My team's 2010-2011 and 2011-2012 seasons were very difficult in terms of wins. We did not have the talent to compete in the Big Ten because as a staff we failed in recruiting. As a seasoned coach and a driven, caring leader, instead of succumbing to frustration, I spent these two seasons mastering how to coach up my players and team. I became a different leader, more understanding, and a better listener. I learned to take responsibility and I also focused on being extremely positive and optimistic. My players were doing the best they could; they competed and worked harder than any one of my teams. They did everything that was asked, but they we were just not as talented and it wasn't their fault.

We spent our energies improving and trying to find ways to compete and to win games. My primary goal was to make sure that my student-athletes had a good experience. We experimented with tactics, we defined winning differently, we set short-term goals, and we celebrated our small successes. In spite of losses on the court, we discovered richer successes could result from striving together to face our challenges with courage and conviction.

Teresa is a CEO and one of my clients. She had just taken over as CEO and was putting the pieces back together within a struggling company. It was overwhelming and nothing seemed to be going right; picking up the pieces, fixing major problems, and putting out fires accounted for 99 percent of her day. To help her combat the challenges, I implemented an approach for celebrating small successes in her daily and weekly routines. Every day, Teresa felt terrible—until she started writing down her small successes on her whiteboard so they were visible. As the whiteboard filled up, she realized she was making tremendous progress. Knowing she was accomplishing something, even small victories, gave her energy, positive affirmation, and visual evidence of her success every day. Today, her company is in a better place and flourishing. Teresa has become more confident in managing and leading her team and her staff has doubled over the past six months.

Leveraging each team member's strengths and coaching them up creates a positive mindset in people. In athletics and business, providing the feedback team members need, the feedback and support they crave, and implementing a driven and caring leadership style are hallmarks of the ON POINT leader.

ONPOINT GAME PLAN: BE A DRIVEN & CARING LEADER

+ Coach your people and teams up and be authentic
+ Let team members know you care about them as people
+ Believe in your people and team; make sure they know it
+ Encourage, empower, and be positive in your words and actions
+ Know when you can challenge, push, and be tough and when to back off
+ Listen to understand
+ Inspire team members to believe they can accomplish more than they think they is possible

---

PART THREE

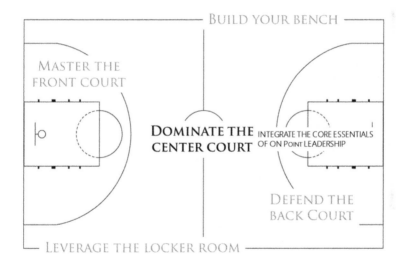

BUILD YOUR BENCH

MASTER THE
FRONT COURT

DOMINATE THE
CENTER COURT

INTEGRATE THE CORE ESSENTIALS
OF ON POINT LEADERSHIP

DEFEND THE
BACK COURT

LEVERAGE THE LOCKER ROOM

ACCEPTING ACCOUNTABILITY

"Accountability—it is not only what we do, but also what we do not do, for which we are accountable."
—Moliere–

I've said it before and I'll say it again: many want to assume the lead role, but few are prepared to accept the responsibility and accountability that go with sitting in that chair. This is not for lack of skill; it's for lack of experience and understanding of what it takes and what is required to be successful as a leader.

Communicating expectations to your team members and then holding them accountable is where most leaders struggle. My goal is to prepare you for this position and the leader's chair (sometimes known as "the hot seat").

President Truman said it best: *The buck stops here.* He had that placard on his desk his entire presidency. Imagine what all of his people thought when they saw this every time they walked in his office. He readily accepted that the authority of his position included the ultimate level of accountability—and that he expected the same from his staff. Truman's strengths represented leadership skills that people could count on from their leader:

- ❖ Making tough decisions

- ❖ Navigating difficult conversations

- ❖ Learning from their failures

- ❖ Providing reassurance and inspiration

- ❖ Taking responsibility and protecting his team

- ❖ Expecting accountability from his team members

SHOULDERING THE WEIGHT

T he 2005-2006 season was my first without an All-American on the team, and I placed unreasonable expectations on players who were not ready. The results speak for themselves—a final record of 19-10 and an NCAA Tournament first-round loss. I saw it coming, and I should have changed its course, but I failed to take back the reins and to communicate directly with the leaders on the team.

What was my mistake? I gave the responsibility to another coaching staff member. To this day, I deeply regret giving this responsibility and power away. We had issues on the team and I gave the responsibility to someone else to solve, to communicate with the captains, and to be the point person.

In looking back, I realize that the players needed ME. I delegated the power to resolve a major ongoing issue when I should have been building this bridge and the relationships with the team's leaders myself. By the end of the season, I was surprised that a number of players were transferring from the program and even the captains were nowhere to be found. All communication lines were shut down and the coaching staff was left standing on an island alone.

Delegating the authority to manage my captains and some of my support staff was one of the biggest mistakes I made as a leader. I put too much pressure on the staff, team, and individual players and, without good leadership within the team, it backfired. Many of my clients delegate people management actions because they don't like to manage people or they choose to avoid it. My experience demonstrates such an approach is a train wreck. Now, I coach my clients on how to manage their staff, to implement regular staff meetings, to communicate openly with their team, and to lead efficiently and effectively.

In the end, I lost five players to transfers and six seniors to graduation. A total of 11 players all in one year—it was devastating. It was "the Perfect Storm" (see Chapter 1). We were extremely successful in previous years and I took my eyes off my strengths: building relationships and communicating effectively with the leaders on the team. We had different leaders than in previous years and I needed to connect and to lead more actively than before. My team was struggling and trying to find their way, but I gave up the most important responsibility a leader could ever have . . . to connect, to listen, and to be there for my team when they needed their head coach the most.

Certainly, conditions that season resulted in a difficult situation. I had student-athletes who were dealing with serious health issues, childhood sexual abuse, and academic ineligibility. Overnight it became culturally acceptable to quit. We were experiencing a perfect storm and quitting was the easy way out. Regardless, I accept my role in the situation and understand that delegating my authority contributed greatly to the problem.

As players departed the program, I took full responsibility for everything that was unfolding; I was the leader and was the one held accountable. I could have avoided the storm by dealing with the issues head-on myself. I didn't see the undermining occurring within my staff and the team. Instead, I delegated and asked my staff to fix it.

From the beginning of the season, without a star player, we needed to win as a collective group, as a team of role players. The season and the team fell apart. The

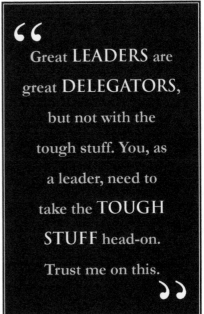

" Great **LEADERS** are great **DELEGATORS,** but not with the tough stuff. You, as a leader, need to take the **TOUGH STUFF** head-on. Trust me on this. "

media was brutal; they exacerbated the situation by reporting about an "internal investigation" when it was actually a routine year-end program review. The administration across campus and within the department already knew the issues within the coaching staff and with the players individually. Unfortunately, my delegation of authority enabled a tough but private situation to explode into an over-blown public scandal.

TAKING THE HEAT

The media market in the Twin Cities is one of—if not the most—vicious media markets in the country. I was the headline in the newspaper and featured in the evening and nighttime news for a long time. The press painted its own picture, sensationalizing the situation. Despite these challenges, this season was a blessing in disguise. I learned so much about people and myself that the experience made me a better leader and an expert in what I do today.

What did I do right? When the situation blew up, I took the blows on behalf of my players. I took responsibility and walked the high road. I didn't expose the personal issues that led to players quitting, and I didn't throw my unprepared team and staff under the bus. I knew I had made a mistake, and it was my job as a leader to protect the players and the program. I didn't hold people I was responsible for accountable during the season, and now I was the one paying the price for the perfect storm. So, I sucked it up and practiced my resiliency as the situation slowly ran out of steam.

What I'm not proud of was the season-long process that I didn't control and for which I didn't take responsibility. I didn't identify concerns and the problems early before they mushroomed. And, I was presumptuous. Presumptuous leadership is dangerous and often produces problems. Our failures were brought about by a lack of leadership, failed communication, and a team strained to perform.

My staff kept saying they had it covered; I was buffered and insulated. Accepting the status quo reports without verification was totally my fault and my isolation was self-imposed. I should have dug into the trenches with my players, instead of putting all the focus on coaching the wins and losses.

What I learned most pointedly is the difference between delegating responsibility and accepting accountability. Yes, I accepted accountability at the end of the year and stood up for the team and the program. I owned the outcome. However, I should have been more present and involved during the process, fulfilling my responsibility as an ON POINT leader to actively guide the team through its challenges.

Executive leaders find that it's lonely at the top. Team leaders and managers also share in this loneliness. Be ready to accept responsibility and to take accountability for every storm you face during your journey. ON POINT leaders know the difference between responsibility and accountability—and exercise both to achieve success.

ON POINT GAME PLAN: ACCEPT ACCOUNTABILITY

+ Delegate responsibility, but with verification and active monitoring
+ Never delegate accountability; always take the heat on the tough stuff (the buck stops with you)
+ Do not place unrealistic pressure and expectations on your team
+ Know what your strengths are and lean on them
+ Hold regular staff meetings and communicate frequently
+ Implement milestones and deadlines for your staff and team
+ Be present; your team needs you in the trenches

THE LOSS OF POWER

"You had the power all along, my dear."
–Glinda, The Good Witch–

Power—I had a lot of it in my position as the head basketball coach at the University of Minnesota. I had the prominent title and status in the community and nationally. I made good money and I had a platform and access to opportunities most don't; my identity was based on what I did for a living.

I know many people in similar privileged positions and some of my closest friends fall into this category. Our identities lie in what we do for a living. Mine did. This is where most of us fall and even fail—whether we admit it or not. We identify others by what they do professionally, and we allow ourselves to be defined by our positions.

Then, on March 28, 2014, my world was rocked. I was let go from my coaching position at Minnesota (see Chapter 6). Released from my program—the one I had built from scratch, several times over. It was devastating; I had just lost my power and, with it, my identity. Being the University of Minnesota head coach defined who I was and was how others identified me: the title, position, influence, and platform. It was gone and I was set adrift. Now what?

POSITIONAL IDENTITY

Power and identity are intertwined. I've watched many people in the coaching profession and in the business world whose sense of self is entirely tied into what they do for a living. Their position is who they are: their identity, their power, and their sense of self-worth. Now, I see it more clearly than ever as I coach and consult with these same individuals.

It's literally devastating to go to bed one night with all that power, then finish the next day with nothing. When it is something you are accustomed to your whole life, it's even more debilitating when suddenly it's gone. Some people handle it well and others don't. Professional athletes retire and, for some, their lives fall apart. It's all they know and they suffer when their power, status, and identities all fall together.

There are many moments—too many to describe—when one distances oneself after losing status, power, and professional identity. For me, some days were good, some days were crushing and emotional, and then other days were refreshing. It's natural for anyone to go through a period of loss and to wonder, *Who am I?* If your identity has been Coach, President, CEO, or Mom your whole life and that position or role is taken away, the first question you face is, *Now what?* I had been Coach my whole life. It was who I am and was my identity my entire life. We all can relate to this personally and/or professionally.

I've talked to hundreds of mothers, fathers, athletes, and business professionals who experience this situation at points in their lives. Most of the time, it represents a major transition during their late forties or early fifties. *Now what? Who am I? What is my purpose? What I have done or what can I do?*

I lost my identity, my power. What I was good at and confident at was taken away, suddenly. My competency in coaching and leading people, guiding a major-college basketball program, managing and leading people, and winning—all were lost in one moment. At the time, I didn't have the perspective to accept one simple fact: someday, every one of us will face such a situation.

Are you ready to lose your power? The answer is this: you will never truly be prepared until it happens. However, the one thing you can do today is to realize what true power is. Do that now. The faster you can learn and develop true power, the easier your transition will be. Trust me; I did it successfully. It wasn't easy and there were many days full of tears, shame, questions, and loneliness.

TRUE POWER

What do I mean by *true* power? What I experienced, after struggling and reflecting, is that true power originates from the inside. It's inside all of us. True power is the authenticity that we embody in our person. Everything we are about resides inside each of us, in our core. Power is personal credibility, self-respect, and integrity to do things the right way. This is true power.

It took me months to figure this out, but once I had recovered my sense of self, I realized I had never lost my power or my identity. I had it the whole time. It was just how I looked at myself and, probably, how others looked at me, too. I never lost my power. The respect, trust, and credibility within ourselves, and within others, is really true power.

In coaching and developing leadership in business, I get many questions from adults who are learning to be true leaders—whether they are leading the company or leading teams. I'd been coaching a team in an influential organization for months, and one of the team members read me the definition of a leader. They asked if I thought the definition was accurate. I replied, *I believe a leader exemplifies many different characteristics—not just a single definition.* They asked, *So, who should be the leader of our team? Shouldn't it be the one who owns a bulk of the business or is the oldest?*

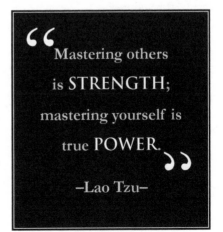

" Mastering others is STRENGTH; mastering yourself is true POWER. "

–Lao Tzu–

Leadership is confusing and hard to understand for many; it's no wonder there are thousands of books about leadership (including this one!). Leadership is a position many want: power, control, and status. It becomes their self-identity and represents how others see them. I have experienced first-hand what great leadership looks like—and what poor leadership looks like when misuse of power, control, and status creates a culture of fear and accumulates advantages to the leader, and to no one else (see Chapter 17).

Power and control are dangerous words and can result in treacherous actions. More often than not, people misuse the two and cause great harm to people, programs, and organizations. In some cases, it can take an organization down, and it can destroy people's lives and livelihoods. Power-abusing people often don't care about those around them, and don't understand their negative effects, because they focus too intently on themselves and on making sure they retain their power and control.

When you have a powerful position and status, everyone wants to be your friend and to be around you. It is a heavy obligation to understand what power is and to know how to use it positively. Instead of making power self-serving, the ON POINT leader's responsibility is to leverage power to serve others. Be a servant leader and use your power to enable others to succeed.

Institutional power comes with a title. But true leadership power may only be earned through respect. The latter can never be taken away from you. The former is easily, and often, wrenched from your grasp. And, when institutional power is taken from you, you truly learn who your friends are, and who makes up your inner circle.

Productive power is not power over people—it's the power to lead and to transform. If others choose to follow, that is effective leadership. Having a bold and inspiring vision, getting buy-in and enabling team alignment, and then executing to drive results is the work of true leaders. That's power.

When I was at the top of my coaching profession, I was building and leading teams that consistently competed in the NCAA Tournament. Everyone wanted a piece of me and my circle was massive. Then, we slipped. We suffered two straight losing seasons with no tournament berths. And, my circle went from massive to microscopic. I learned to be very cautious in trusting and getting close to people. I learned to become intuitive and to excel at reading people and their intentions.

Have you ever lost your power or identity, as a coach, parent, manager, or CEO? Are you afraid that you will? Someday, we all will lose what we consider our power and identity. It's what you do next that counts.

POWER IN TRANSITION

Have you lost your job or are you transitioning personally or professionally? If not, at some point in your life, you will. Transitioning careers, losing relationships, retiring, or sending your kids off to college—these are all major life transitions that are bound to happen to you.

Transitioning into the management or executive level, or from a vice president to a president's role, requires a major shift in mindset and approach for managing and leading others. Recognize the difference and take action to advance your leadership presence. You must be ON POINT and lift your mindset and approach to the next level. More will be expected of you.

As a leader, you also will need to expect more from others. Those around you will look to you to make decisions and to solve problems all day, every day. You will need to influence, inspire, and understand your peers and direct reports. They will all view you through a different lens because you have a title and more power. Don't misuse it; all eyes will be on you, expecting you to perform and to be consistent, and some will be waiting for you to fail.

When I was an assistant coach, I thought I knew it all. Most assistants and subordinates think that they can do it better and would do it differently. However, if anyone could do it, then why aren't more doing it? When I accepted the opportunity to be a head coach on two different occasions, I thought I had it all figured out. Like many others who came before me, I learned it wasn't as easy as I thought. Sitting in that chair and changing my title, power, and responsibility caused a monumental shift for me personally and professionally—and for those around me.

It will take patience when you're at the pinnacle of an organization or in your career. Moving into the head coaching role for me took determination, support, and mentoring to navigate the life transition. I made it a priority to surround myself with the right people.

Power can be addictive, but it doesn't have to be. My long-time athletic director, my mentor, kept me grounded every day. He always reminded me to stay the course and to remember where I came from. He would remind me all the time that I grew up on a farm in Ohio, had a truly substantive upbringing, and developed steadfast values growing up. Don't ever lose sight of who you are at the core—this is true power. Don't ever lose yourself in all of your success.

From the beginning of my coaching career to March 28, 2014, was the blink of an eye and suddenly I was faced with transitioning out of 27 years of college coaching. This was a loss of power, but truly not a loss of true power. I have always leaned on and relied on my mentors throughout my career. Some mentors have come and gone; I developed new ones and stayed connected to old ones.

Ten days after my last day at the University of Minnesota, one of my mentors called and requested a meeting. I drove to the tallest building in downtown Minneapolis, took the elevator up to the office, and was escorted to an ornate conference room overlooking the beautiful cityscape of Minneapolis.

I knew this meeting would be different. Indeed, it changed the course of my life. My mentor placed an entire pad of paper and a pen in front of me. We had a long heart-to-heart conversation like never before. We discussed what I wanted to do with the rest of my life and how I would respond during my transition. We talked about my passions and where I saw myself in five to 10 years. My mentor offered one of the most substantive compliments and pieces of advice I have ever received: *You're a recognized leader, stay visible and relevant.*

To this day, I often find myself reviewing the notes I took that day. After a nearly three-hour meeting, I was ready for the next chapter of my life to begin. I was ready to put college athletics behind and I was ready and willing to prepare for what lay ahead. I was ready to stay visible and relevant, and prepared to take my leadership expertise to another level.

When one door closes, another will surely open. At this moment, a beautiful and memorable door closed and a big and bold, French, triple-paned door opened. I was ready to walk through it and make the next chapter of my life as successful as the one I had just left. I decided to become an entrepreneur, a business owner.

The light bulb went off and it made perfect sense for me. I love to coach and develop people. My entire life I pushed, challenged, managed, and led people and teams. I was successful doing it and I learned so much from all the challenges along the way. I had seen it all and experienced what most would only read about or see on realty television. I benefited from an executive coach during my tenure coaching in the Big Ten, I had a great experience, I learned a lot about myself, became self-aware, and I realized this transition was a perfect fit and a natural progression of my skills. I was going to be . . . a coach!

Yes, the loss of power and my identity felt devastating for a full year, but I learned what true power is. I realized I never lost my power or my identity because, all along, I stayed true to myself and kept my dignity and integrity. I was respected and trusted in the community and on a national level. I realized that my core and my authentic self positioned me to offer even more as an ON POINT leader. Today, I bring these powerful values to my coaching and consulting clients and organizations. This is the true power of being ON POINT and, even more importantly, it is truly who I am: a coach.

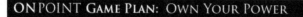

ONPOINT GAME PLAN: OWN YOUR POWER

+ Be ready; losing power will happen to you in one form or another
+ Understand what true power is; it's inside of you
+ Never lose your integrity; it is all you have
+ Never underestimate the damage that misusing one's power and control can do to people's lives
+ Understand that true power involves leading and transforming others through respect and credibility
+ Know that when one door closes, another door opens
+ Stay true to yourself and you will never lose your true power

TAKING RISKS

"A ship is always safe at the shore—
but that is NOT what it is built for."
—Albert Einstein—

I have been asked by many people to write or to speak about leadership and risk-taking, especially for women. When I stop and think about these topics and what risks I have taken during my personal and professional life, I realize I have taken more risks than I thought.

RISK'S REWARDS

Reflecting on my early childhood, I have always been a risk-taker. Some have been worth it and others I have learned from and were mistakes. My risk-taking started early growing up on a farm and riding dirt bikes, driving snowmobiles, and operating heavy machinery—I lived on the edge and flirted with danger routinely. In taking risks growing up, I learned a lot about myself and I pushed myself beyond limits I never knew I faced. I loved speed, thrived on adventure, was comfortable taking risks; I experienced failure and learned at an early age to move on to the next play in life, never delaying too long in any one moment.

In a small community, families tend to stay near home and to live near each other. I was the first one of my siblings to go to a four-year college and then moved away from home to the east coast to take my first job at the age of 22. I was considered the black sheep in the family and the one who wasn't afraid to take risks.

Moving to the east coast, I spent nine years at the University of Vermont, first as an assistant and then as the head coach. After nine years, I was successful and comfortable in Burlington, but I was only 31 years old and I wanted more. I wanted to be at an institution and with a program with a chance to go to a Final Four and to win a national championship. We couldn't achieve that at Vermont. So, I took a professional risk and stepped back in the hope that eventually I would land a head-coaching job in one of the top five conferences in the country.

Leaving Vermont, I accepted an assistant coaching position at Boston College. I struggled for a few weeks and obsessed about making the right decision. I was worried about what everyone would think and I wondered if the move would help me accomplish my goals. I accepted the risk and took what most considered a step backwards, joining Boston College as an assistant. In three years, I was promoted to associate head coach and eventually was recruited and hired at the University of Minnesota as head basketball coach.

Leaving Vermont involved risk-taking and the decision was one I anguished over. But I made the decision and was optimistic and approached it as a win-win, no matter what happened. The risk paid off five years later when I landed a big-time job in the best and richest conference in the country, the Big Ten. This risk, and others in my life, have paid off and propelled me to greater heights. In addition, success in accepting risk gave me more confidence to continue taking more risks.

The greater the risk, the greater the reward—we've all heard this saying—and it was a common refrain from many people who were close to me. As a head coach, it felt like every year I was hiring people for assistant positions, securing new support staff and, of course, recruiting players. Several times while hiring my staff, I was torn between two people. On a few occasions I choose the wrong one, trying to select what I thought was the "less risky" candidate. I was being careful and didn't want to make a mistake, so I played it safe more times than I want to admit. Some of these choices turned out just fine and some didn't. What I learned is that I am an expert in hiring people and putting teams together, so I should trust myself and take the risk on a person if I felt it would benefit me and my team.

I also took risks on the types of student-athletes I recruited. Some of these risks did not turn out so well. When you sacrifice values and what you look for in the people you surround yourself with, in a brutal and results-driven profession, too many mistakes will cost you your job. You need to select people who will perform on and off the floor: those who would fit your style, personality, and expectations and those who could compete in the Big Ten and at the University of Minnesota, academically, socially, and athletically. I took risks in recruiting that set the program back.

Today, I'm surrounded by the best! My board members, my business partners, the people who run my organizations, my clients, and my friends all have these characteristics and traits. I learned the hard way but now, in my own businesses and in life, these are the only types of people I hire, work with, or have on my teams.

Deciding to leave college basketball coaching after 27 years to start my own business represented a huge risk. People thought I was crazy. College coaches looked at me and said, *All you/we know how to do is coach basketball.* True, we had played and coached basketball our whole lives and to think about doing something else was scary and daunting.

Recently, I spoke to one of my greatest mentors who still coaches the game today. He has coached for more than 30 years and is in the Hall of Fame. He said to me, *I thought all we could ever do was coach basketball. But look at what you have done. You transferred all of your skills of managing, leading, coaching, and motivating, and you took those skills into coaching and consulting in business and corporate America.* Many of my

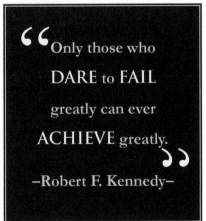

"Only those who DARE to FAIL greatly can ever ACHIEVE greatly.

–Robert F. Kennedy–

clients are former high school or college athletes and/or have children who play sports. They relate to how athletics teaches lessons for tackling tough business problems and prevailing when faced with adversity. They get it more quickly, and understand it more deeply, than most.

It's in an organization's best interest to combine lessons from athletics for managing change in universities and in business. If you're too slow to adapt to changes taking place in the university and collegiate athletics environment, the entire enterprise will come tumbling down. In business, if you're too slow to change or you don't manage change effectively or quickly, you'll find yourself and your organization disjointed while the competition is winning and moving light years ahead.

FEAR AND COMFORT

For many people, risk-taking is way outside of their comfort zone. We are most comfortable staying in our box and comfort zones for our entire personal and professional lives. Unfortunately, if we don't break away from safe and secure habits, we won't grow and advance. Are you at the same place you were 10 to 15 years ago and feeling stale or stagnant in your life or career? If so, you need to take some risks.

If the fear of taking a risk holds you back, understand that staying in your comfort zone and avoiding change carries a cost as well. When considering a risk, keep in mind four key points that are the staples of successful risk-takers (I have found them to be mine):

1. *Your comfort zone is all in your mind.* If you stay in your comfort zone and resist change out of fear—of failure, success, or rejection—you won't accomplish all you want or reach your full potential. Your comfort zone is a mindset and a place you choose to "protect" yourself. And, like all mindsets, you can choose to change it—NOW!

2. *Fear is not a function of courage, but a lack of confidence.* Challenge yourself with these questions: What am I afraid of? Are my fears realistic? Will I ignore these anxieties and combat them? What's the worst thing that could happen? What do I have to lose? Then break it down and take action.

3. *You learn more from the losses and failures than you do from the wins and successes.* The losses test our capabilities mentally and emotionally. They can provide the most important learning you will ever experience. They help us grow and provide new insight we might not have gained any other way. As long as you maintain your confidence and keep self-doubt from creeping in, future risk-taking becomes easier and eventually will deliver your greatest reward.

4. *Choose to be the best!* No one tells us how broad and deep our comfort zone is. The choice to take risks is ours. Examine the mindset that holds you back, then decide to open a new door that can help lead you to your passions and to your purpose as an ON POINT leader.

If you're comfortable, get uncomfortable and push yourself to grow. Meet new people, seek new experiences, or learn a new skill. Scan the environment and find a way to get out of your box, to get uncomfortable, and to take some risks. It will feel disconcerting and, at times, you may struggle with confidence. ON POINT leaders experience rewards and accomplish things they never thought they would when they take risks.

ON POINT GAME PLAN: TAKE RISKS

+ Realize it's safe to take risks and get out of your comfort zone

+ Identify what you are afraid of, weigh all options, then take action

+ Decide if you want to be the best; if so, do something about it

+ Take a small step you would consider a risk, then keep raising the bar

+ Ask yourself: *What is the worst thing that could happen?*

+ Have the confidence to live your life to the fullest; live your passions and find your purpose

MANAGING
CHANGE

"The greatest danger in times of turbulence is not the turbulence—
it is to act with yesterday's logic."
—Peter Drucker—

I received a text message one evening from a company's president—
he had accepted a new, significant job in the market in which I lived.
He was new to the area and, as an experienced and highly successful leader,
was given the task of entering the market and changing what had been broken for many years. This leader was told to "fix it" and do it fast.

The text asked if I would be willing to have a conversation about managing change and if I would be someone they could talk to, collaborate with,
and ensure their compass and rudder pointed in the right direction. Bringing someone in from the outside with a fresh perspective, with a new set
of eyes and ears, and with independence has been valuable to the leader.
Today, the leader has been in the organization for over a year and a half
and change is rampant. It's been a journey of onward, upward, across, and
down the organization very quickly.

I continue to work with and collaborate with this leader and it's been
amazing to see the positive change. There's a clear vision, a plan in place,
and more buy-in than ever before; he empowered others to lead and
raised the level of expectations and accountability with people and teams
within the organization.

CHANGE OR FAIL

Transformation and managing change don't happen overnight; there are multiple actions and conditions that need to occur quickly for executives to experience positive forward movement. It's also critical that people in the organization understand that what happened in the past doesn't work and that changes must be made.

Managing change is a constant across all industries, athletic departments and professional sports organizations, programs, and project teams. Some industries, such as technology, media, finance, and healthcare experience an even greater pace of change.

Many leaders are unprepared to act on and to create an environment necessary for change and transformation. For many organizations, preparedness begins at the top and this means that leadership at all levels must have a shared vision, undeniable clarity in purpose and focus, and alignment in strategy and goals. Unfortunately, many organizations are slow to change as internal politics hinder buy-in at all levels of leadership—even when the need for change is immediate, obvious, and critical. This is why many organizations and teams lose momentum and can't implement change fast enough, allowing competitors to outperform them and, ultimately, hastening the departure of leader(s) at the top.

I have led through and managed times of change throughout my career, in many different scenarios. My industry and my role changed over the course of my career, from being a basketball coach to becoming a CEO of my program and running a business, all while facing public scrutiny. The world of college athletics changed under my feet and the landscape and the expectations shifted continually. No one handed me a manual, and I wasn't taught change management in my college courses, but I had to learn it on the job—by actually doing it and transforming my role and my career virtually overnight.

To manage change successfully, it is imperative that the ON POINT leader have a clear vision of and alignment to the following questions:

What does success look like—and how does this benefit our people, clients, and stakeholders?

What problem or solution is our mission trying to fulfill for the industry we serve—and how can we sustain our success and improve our ability to accomplish more than in the past?

What must the organization and program do to remain competitive, become more profitable, retain top talent, and/or become the best or an expert in the industry?

What resources and relationships are necessary to accomplish our goals and to achieve sustainable success?

It's easy for leaders to say that they need to improve and to invest in doing things better because most of the time, the industry or their bosses are expecting results or they are being proactive. The reality is that change is a long journey to failure without a defined vision, clear goals, actionable strategy, and organizational buy-in. Many people and leaders have a compelling idea or vision, but without the right strategy, alignment, and execution, the vision won't become a reality. When leaders travel this path, their credibility suffers, their vision and plan are questioned, and doubt begins to set in with the people and teams around them.

Many senior-level executives know this, yet are not sufficiently skilled or willing to take the time to build necessary relationships they need to make it happen. They may focus entirely on the execution of the transformation but when teams face adversity, and they always will, they may not have a collaborative and tight-knit, high-performing team that will survive a perfect storm together.

When asked what keeps leaders up at night, those involved in managing change often say they are concerned about how their people and teams will react, how they can get everyone on the same page working together as a team, and

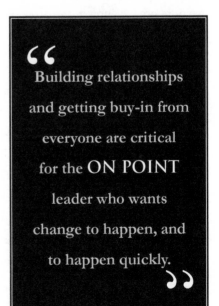

> **Building relationships and getting buy-in from everyone are critical for the ON POINT leader who wants change to happen, and to happen quickly.**

how they will be able to lead their people and teams. They wonder if people will follow, they worry about being liked, and they are concerned that their leadership style won't be successful in bringing everyone together.

Instead, they should focus on the organization's values and emphasize creating a culture of commitment and leadership development. Leaders who fail don't think about or plan for the people side of change and they often find themselves wondering what happened. They fail by only looking at the operations, the execution side, and they don't spend time building the relationships that, ultimately, are the difference-maker for change—especially when facing times of adversity.

PLAYBOOK FOR CHANGE

No single approach fits every organization or situation, but fundamental strategies and approaches can be used in many situations. The following 10 principles are the key elements in a playbook for managing change. Using these as a guide, game plan, or framework, executive leaders can understand what to expect, how to manage personal change in how they lead, and how to engage their people and the entire organization in the process.

1. *Build Relationships.* Develop meaningful and authentic relationships. Any significant change creates "people" issues. New leaders will be expected to be ON POINT, jobs and roles will change, leadership skills must be developed, and employees and teams will be skeptical and resistant. Lacking a proactive approach or authentic leadership style will put leaders behind the eight-ball immediately. Dealing with these issues on a reactive basis puts speed, morale, and a high success rate at risk. A proactive approach and a plan for managing change—beginning with the leader, addressing the leadership team, and then building relationships with key stakeholders—should be developed out of the gate. Make sure to practice agility as change moves through the organization or team.

2. *Start With the One ON POINT.* Change is uncomfortable at all levels of an organization or during a major project, but at the end of the day, all

eyes turn toward the leader, the CEO, and the leadership team for vision, inspiration, and direction. The leaders must embrace change first so they may challenge and motivate the rest of the team and organization. They all must speak with one voice and inspire with the vision of where they are going and what they will accomplish together. Achieving leadership alignment requires significant support during times of high expectations and high stress.

Leadership teams that work as a tight-knit group turn out to be high-performing teams and are best positioned for success. They are aligned and committed to the leader and the direction of change. It's important they understand the culture and the direction of change so they can also message those changes themselves.

3. *Connect Everyone.* Change involves communicating a vision and strategy that affects all levels of the organization. Managing change must include the leader identifying other leaders and delegating responsibility, so others are empowered and change becomes contagious and invigorating throughout the organization. At each layer of the organization, leaders must be aligned, prepared to execute the strategy, and motivated to make change happen.

A successful ON POINT leader communicates the vision and the leadership team helps set the goals, strategy, and targets as a collaborative team. Next, more of the organization's leaders and managers help design the change initiative, beginning to spread collaboration and connection more broadly. Connecting everyone is a significant catalyst for

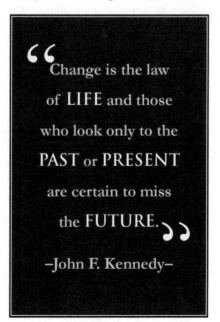

" Change is the law of **LIFE** and those who look only to the **PAST** or **PRESENT** are certain to miss the **FUTURE.** "

–John F. Kennedy–

implementation. In addition, this approach paves the way to leader succession and helps identify and prepare the next generation of leadership.

4. *Share an Inspiring Vision.* Individuals will question change; they will challenge the company's direction and decide if they want to commit personally to making change happen. An inspiring vision will help individuals and teams buy into you, the ON POINT leader, and to take the first, tentative steps to support change. Follow three steps in developing the vision. First, confront the reality of the culture and communicate an inspiring need for change. Leaders must customize their message internally, communicating the opportunity for change to create passion in people Second, demonstrate your belief that the organization has a promising future and the leadership to get there. Finally, provide a game plan and the resources to get it done.

5. *Generate Ownership and Listen.* Leaders of large-scale change must over-achieve during the process and create support for change among their people. This requires more than mere acceptance or passive head nods of agreement. It demands ownership by leaders willing to accept responsibility for making change happen in all of the areas they influence. Ownership results from involving and listening to others when identifying problems and providing solutions.

Executives or team leaders need to work with their teams to learn more and to get further exposure to changes that need to occur. Many times, listening and getting participation are the turning points and enable change transitions to happen quickly. Learning also creates an environment for top executives to work together as a team, enabling alignment and a level of teamwork that groups rarely experience.

6. *Communicate, Then Communicate More.* Too often, change leaders make the mistake of assuming that others understand the issues, believe that change needs to happen, and see the direction they are all heading. I learned to never assume anything, not even the obvious. The best leaders through change communicate regularly and timely, and they do a lot of listening. Communications and ideas flow up from the bottom, in from the middle, and out from the top, and are targeted to provide everyone information at the right time and to give everyone an opportunity for input and feedback. Success in managing change requires over-communication using a variety of methods and involving everyone.

7. *Assess and Evaluate the Culture.* Managing change picks up speed and intensity with progress and success. To keep pace, it is critical that leaders understand the culture and sensitivities at each level of the organization and recognize that culture operates most distinctly and forcefully at the workplace's front lines.

Organizations often make the mistake of assessing culture either too late or not at all. Evaluating the culture can assess readiness to change, bring major problems to the surface, identify issues, and highlight the areas of resistance. Cultural assessment will identify the values, beliefs, and perceptions that must be taken into account for successful change to occur. As important as the vision and buy-in, these cultural conditions are essential fundamentals needed to drive change. Everyone must be on the bus and prepared to move in the same direction, and culture is the bus driver.

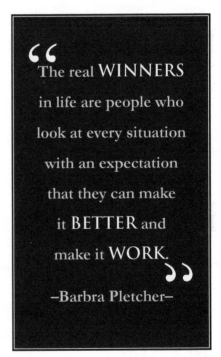

" The real WINNERS in life are people who look at every situation with an expectation that they can make it BETTER and make it WORK. "

–Barbra Pletcher–

8. *Reinforce the Culture.* Progress in managing change can be undone by culture. Once cultural expectations are communicated, culture should be addressed as often as any other area in change management. Leaders should be precise about the expectations that will drive and support change, and then consistently model and reward those behaviors. Establishing a healthy and functional culture is a key ingredient in designing a change management game plan.

Successfully managing change can involve developing a culture, combining cultures, or reinforcing cultures. I have led through all three scenarios and experienced them in the non-leadership role. I have seen leaders combine cultures effectively and I have seen leaders fail by sabotaging a healthy culture and turning it toxic. It starts and stops with the one ON POINT. Know that you have a choice: design and nurture the culture you desire . . . or struggle with the culture that thrives in the vacuum.

9. *Prepare for the Unexpected.* When managing change, game plans often do not go as planned. People react differently, skeptics resist change, and external stakeholders shift. Effectively managing and leading change requires continual assessment and evaluation of its impact and the organization's willingness to adapt to new expectations. An effective change management plan identifies potential barriers and anticipates circumstances that may arise. Good leaders are agile and can make the adjustments necessary to maintain momentum and to drive results.

10. *Engage With Your People and Teams.* Change is a process and a journey. People spend many more hours at work than with their families at home. Think of your colleagues as family. Individuals and teams need effective communication at all times. They need to know how their work will change, what is expected during and after the change, how their performance will be measured, and how team success or failure is measured. Team leaders should be transparent, open, and vulnerable. People will react to what they see and hear around them every time. Praise and reinforce those who are doing a great job and staying the course. Removing those who stand in the way of change will reinforce the organization's commitment and give the team freedom to succeed.

ON POINT leaders involved in managing change know that the people matter the most. It is tempting for leaders to dwell on all the processes, which are linear and rational, rather than handle conflict, build relationships, and take care of critical people issues. Mastering the people side of change should not be a mystery but a priority.

CHANGE IS A TEAM SPORT

Leadership must break down silos across functional/departmental areas in order to stimulate change and transformation in programs and organizations. Organizations should reinforce collaboration and inspire innovative teams to solve problems and to identify opportunities together. Teamwork trumps everything and, without it, nothing else matters. A high level of communication and understanding supports an expectation that only team players belong in the organization and fit the culture. High-performing teams challenge each other and advance their ideals together as one team. Functioning alone on an island with no respect for the team is not acceptable.

As you think about your own organization, is everyone clear about the organization's vision, expectations, and goals? Do they have the mindset and attitude that are expected to support change? Many organizations and leaders fail because they fail to achieve alignment and that makes change very difficult. Communication and the ability to define clear expectations and direction is a step that can't be assumed. This is why silos exist in every organization—forcing change management upon itself and its employees.

It's impossible for an organization and teams to achieve alignment when the leadership teams within a company represent disjointed parts. High-performing teams are in sync and are connected. Managing change becomes a challenge when leaders across the organization do not work together as a team, communicate with one another, share and challenge each other's ideas, and serve as each other's biggest fans. If one silo fails, the organization, team, project, and individual fails.

Be the ON POINT leader who thrives in an environment of constant change and create an environment of trust, alignment, and transparency. You won't make change easy, but you will pave a pathway to success for your organization, team, and team members.

ONPOINT GAME PLAN: MANAGE CHANGE

+ Build relationships and connect everyone
+ Share an inspiring vision, then build ownership and get others invested in the direction
+ Listen to others' experiences, ideas, and opinions
+ Communicate in a timely and effective fashion (then over-communicate)
+ Assess and evaluate the culture, then create a health culture of teamwork
+ Prepare for the unexpected
+ Engage with your people and teams; people matter the most!
+ Create an environment of trust and transparency

BUILDING A
BUSINESS PERSONA

*"A strong, positive self-image is the best possible
preparation for success in life."*
—Dr. Joyce Brothers—

**Everywhere I turn, top leaders of companies express the need for
women in their organizations to be coached and developed in the
areas of executive presence and gravitas**. These key attributes hold
many women back from getting to the next level.

According to a recent study from the Center for Talent Innovation, 268
senior executives cited executive presence, or being perceived as leadership material, as an essential component to getting ahead. And, 67 percent of senior executives cited that confidence is the core characteristic
of executive presence. You do not have to be a loud leader, toot your own
horn, brag, or talk a big story; it's how you carry yourself and how you
walk into a room and own it.

DEFINING "IT"

t the executive level, women represent only 14.6 percent of executive
officers according to The Women in Leadership Gap. Obviously, that
means more than 85 percent of these positions are filled with men.

Many women in high-potential positions are skilled, talented, connected, emotionally intelligent, and respected—but many are missing what organizations look for in those positions. They are missing "IT."

Executive presence may be difficult to define, but we know "IT" when we see it. When people with "IT" walk into a room, heads turn. Everyone wants to have a conversation with them, people get up and out of their chairs, all eyes go on them, and conversations are directed toward them. When they speak, people listen. When they are up on stage, they have stage presence. When they lead, people follow.

I have been asked on many occasions, and often by men, to explain how can they coach, develop, and mentor women on their executive presence. Women work hard, they are brilliant, they receive promotions, and they are in the group next in line to become a president of the company. A male president of a company approached me and said, *Pam, I don't know how to say it, what to do, and I feel like I have to talk to women differently than I talk to men.*

A main ingredient and the icing on the cake is executive presence, especially for women. Where is your confidence level today and do you have the courage to sit in that chair and go to the next level? I have attended a variety of events ranging from meetings, galas, black tie events, and rubber-chicken dinners with top-level executives from every industry—men and women. What holds many, and may I say most women, back in their professional growth is a lack of confidence and courage.

While coaching at the University of Minnesota I was expected to attend fundraisers and black tie events and I learned quickly that it was important to engage in the community, to become part of the Twin Cities and the state of Minnesota, and to build trust and credibility. Most people don't understand that success required more than just winning basketball games. I understood how important it was for me to have executive presence and gravitas to connect with people and to help them hear and to believe my message.

I needed to connect with people in a variety of industries to build a platform, credibility, and trust. I developed executive presence quickly for people to hear my message, to believe in me, and to endorse what I was doing. I enjoyed it and connected easily with people, learning to build trust rapidly. I attended many events with the "who's who" crowd and mastered the art of scanning a crowd and working a room.

I gravitate to those people who demonstrate executive presence and gravitas because they are the ones who can make a difference. They have the ability to command a room. They are engaging with people, actively listening, and exemplify authenticity. The ones who stand in the corner, sitting in the same chair all night, and look uncomfortable are those individuals I get questions about from the "85 percent men" at the executive level.

DEVELOPING "IT"

There are three characteristics I look for to characterize executive presence: Confidence, Communication, and Appearance. As you read on, evaluate yourself and take note of how you may improve your executive presence.

CONFIDENCE:
Substance, Composure, Self-Assurance, Resonance, and Competence

Carry yourself with the confidence and assurance that you own the room. You may be walking into a room full of men and high-level executives, it may be a black tie event, you may not know anyone, and you may even be an introvert— but you can command a room and people will notice you immediately without saying a word.

The way you carry yourself will say it all; it's an art and will take you far. You may be nervous and not know anyone, but walk, move, and demonstrate a level of energy that exudes confidence and self-assurance. Your energy, laughter, smile, and the way you glide around the room will say it all.

Have confidence in yourself, believe in what you are doing, understand your strengths, and recognize that there are many attributes you should love about yourself. For almost three decades working with student-athletes, it was my responsibility to develop and to instill confidence in others: to lift people up, to help them to realize their strengths, and to convince them that they could achieve their wildest dreams. First, you need to like yourself, to believe in yourself, to like what you see in the mirror, and to have the confidence that you will succeed.

Look for activities that feed your confidence. I have found a passion in Bikram yoga and I attend sessions regularly. Yoga has the ability to connect you with yourself, to calm your thoughts, and to become mindful of appreciating yourself. There's a women who attends regularly and I can see her in the long mirror of the yoga room. When our instructor tells us to look into our own eyes in the mirror, connecting with ourselves, this woman never looks at herself in the mirror. Never. Instead, she stares directly at the floor. She just can't look at herself in the mirror. I assume she feels uncomfortable with herself, has a lack of confidence, doesn't like what she sees, and would rather not look into her own eyes. I only hope she is different and exudes confidence outside the yoga studio at home and in the workplace. But, for some reason, I don't think that's true. Can you stand in front of the mirror and look directly into your own eyes? Try it.

Do you project confidence in your meetings with your peers, bosses, clients, and your direct reports? One of my clients is a senior-level executive and she said, *Pam, I know I shouldn't feel this way but I'm in meetings all day with men. As soon as I walk through that doorway and sit down, I start questioning myself on why am I there and I lose my confidence right away.* I looked her straight in the eye and said, *There is a reason you are a senior-level executive and in that room and in that chair. You work hard and you deserve to be there. If, at any point, you start to question that, you can never, ever show it. Don't ever give your confidence away to anyone.* She looked at me with new confidence in her eyes and said, *You're absolutely right!*

At Minnesota, my point guard was my leader who was ON POINT everyday no matter what. She ran the team, called the plays, knew where everyone was supposed to be on the floor, brought calm, and knew everyone's strengths as players. Everyone looked to the point guard to be ON POINT. When situations got tense, and they were often, everyone looked to the team's leaders: the point guard and me. If we didn't look confident or in control, we risked losing our team immediately. The same thing happens in the business world.

COMMUNICATION:
Effective, Knowledgeable, Relevant, Professional, Engaging, Active Listener

Make what you say and do match who you are. Listen to others intently, engage emotionally, be approachable, and demonstrate interest and concern. Communication is the foundation for building trust and credibility. As you listen to an ON POINT leader communicate, you can see and experience these attributes. When people see and listen to effective leaders in action, they want to follow. Learn to say the right thing, at the right time, and learn to avoid saying the wrong thing during an emotional or stressful moment.

Having great speaking skills, being an effective communicator, exercising assertiveness, and mastering the ability to read an audience or situation are critical communication skills. According to a recent study from the Center for Talent Innovation, 28 percent of executives (your bosses) felt that good communication telegraphs that you are leadership material. If you are someone who does not speak up in staff meetings, has no voice or opinion, are too politically correct, and don't speak with confidence, you will be minimized in your role. You choose.

How are you communicating, what are you saying, what is being heard, and what is revealed on the other end of a conversation? Executive presence means sounding competent in your field and commanding attention through the language you use. Sounding educated is essential if you want to rise to the next level. Unprofessional speech detracts from one's executive presence.

It's also important to stay relevant in your industry and up-to-date on current news and events; this supports an ability to start and to hold a conversation with other executives. At every event I attend, I move from table to table to say hello and I try to connect with as many people I can in the room. Be the one who initiates the conversation and engages. People will respond to you and placing yourself in an assertive position will build your confidence.

Too many times I hear that women don't accept a promotion or don't want to go to the next level in a president or C-suite position because they are not ready. A senior-level leader I know turned down an offer to consider one of these positions. I asked her, *What were you thinking? What do you mean you're not ready—when have any one of us ever been ready for a big job?* Don't wait for all your T's to be crossed and I's dotted; it doesn't work like that. You will wait for a very long time because you will never be ready. Significant, meaningful positions always require learning on the job.

In turning down opportunities, are you afraid to take risks, afraid to fail, or lack confidence? If you're ever in this position, tighten your seat belt, strap in, lace up your shoes, and take the job. All you're doing is sabotaging yourself before taking the position. If you think you're not ready, please don't say it out loud. Just take the position—you may never get the opportunity again and I guarantee you will regret it.

APPEARANCE:
Stylish, Assertive, Engaging, Inclusive, and Professional

Stay true to you, but when we're talking about executive presence and gravitas, how you dress and your appearance does not go unnoticed. Confidence and your appearance go hand in hand. We all feel more confident when we get those sweat pants off and put on our business or gala attire.

You do not need to wear expensive clothes or jewelry but, according to a recent study from the Center for Talent Innovation, executives examine one's appearance for executive presence. They look for demonstration of professionalism: that one looks put together and looks the part. I know what you might be thinking, but it truly matters how you dress, how you wear your hair, and how you apply your makeup. This will set you apart from the mid-level management positions to the executive level. I recommend you over-dress rather than under-dress, every time. You only have one opportunity to make a first impression and it could be your last. Your hair, nails, fitness, and fit of clothing matter. Are you wearing your power suit? Remember, we are talking about executive presence and gravitas; your appearance, and how others see you, can make a difference.

What is expected in your workplace and culture? Does your organization allow people to wear jeans and sweatshirts, where staff members arrive unshaven and sloppy to work? I have been to events and the leaders have shown up un-showered and unshaven, wearing a hooded sweatshirt and oversized jeans. Need I say more?! Remember, investing in your leadership and executive presence, for both men and women, pays dividends.

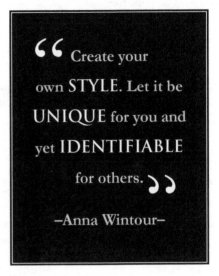

" Create your own STYLE. Let it be UNIQUE for you and yet IDENTIFIABLE for others. "

–Anna Wintour–

The good news is that executive presence can be learned and improved. This is and should be a major part of your growth. If you are not continuing to grow and you're too comfortable, get out of your comfort zone. How are you going to reach your goals? Everything you get—a promotion, an award, a raise, a job—must be earned. No one will give you anything and don't expect it to be easy.

While there are many more elements to create executive presence, looking, acting, thinking, and communicating like a leader are essential. I love coaching, supporting, and instilling the confidence needed in my clients to reach their full potential. When it comes to executive presence, remember that actions speak louder than words. So, take the time to think through these tips and be aware of how those around you perceive you.

If you don't know where to start on executive presence, get a coach or ask your boss to be your mentor. Work on one skill at a time, then build your full business persona gradually and steadily. Have confidence in yourself and believe! Your ON POINT persona awaits.

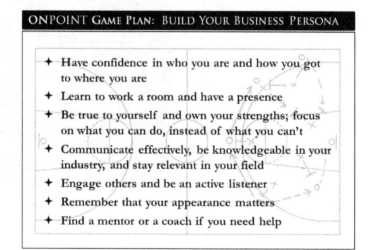

ONPOINT GAME PLAN: BUILD YOUR BUSINESS PERSONA

+ Have confidence in who you are and how you got to where you are
+ Learn to work a room and have a presence
+ Be true to yourself and own your strengths; focus on what you can do, instead of what you can't
+ Communicate effectively, be knowledgeable in your industry, and stay relevant in your field
+ Engage others and be an active listener
+ Remember that your appearance matters
+ Find a mentor or a coach if you need help

THE X-FACTOR: EMOTIONAL INTELLIGENCE

"If you are tuned out of your own emotions, you will be poor at reading them in other people."
–Daniel Goleman–

Effective leaders lead with emotional intelligence. They have the skills to manage and to use their emotions to benefit themselves, to understand and to support others, and to enrich their organization's culture. And, like all leadership skills, emotional skills can be learned and developed. Much of this is learned through experience.

THE NEW INTELLIGENCE

The more we act a certain way—happy, depressed, optimistic, or pessimistic—the more the behavior becomes ingrained, and the more we will continue to feel and act that way on a daily basis. I often think to myself, I am an eternal optimist and that is how I look at my life and my work. I am full of positive energy and go into every environment with the mindset to inspire and empower people. That is the expectation I have set for myself and I accept it.

Academics have researched interpersonal behavior for several decades, and coined the term emotional intelligence (EI). Business leaders quickly leveraged the concept and made EI their own, immediately grasping its relevance and importance to the workplace and to effective leadership. Your EI quotient includes your personal qualities such as perseverance, self-control, and influence through building relationships. Hiring managers are wise to look for high EI skills and competences in people; it is truly the X-factor.

A few of my clients were frustrated with co-workers because they were not getting things done or things were not getting done in a timely fashion. Meetings were rescheduled and their priorities were put at the bottom of the pile. I asked, *Do you have a good relationship with your co-workers? Do you talk to them other than when you want something from them? Have you thanked them for all they do?* They admitted practicing none of these behaviors. I told them that they needed to develop a relationship. Learn to influence without authority. Stop by their office and say hello, go to lunch, send them a thank you note, ask them what you can do for them, and make them feel important. If you can do this authentically, you will find that your co-workers will fit you into their schedule that same day, your request will rise to the top of the pile, and they will go the extra mile.

I'm passionate about the concept of EI and how it influences the work environment. To me, it is as critical, if not more critical, than technical skills because it supersedes culture. Studies suggest four key components of EI: self-awareness, self-management, social awareness, and relationship management.

SELF-AWARENESS

EI starts with self-assessment to gain a healthy understanding of one's strengths and weaknesses. In addition, awareness must include a comprehensive understanding of how your actions affect others. Self-aware people excel in a constructive environment that features upward and downward feedback. The confidence from high self-awareness helps the individual and their team.

Leaders can become self-aware by seeing themselves through the eyes of those around them. Hearing the truth can be difficult, but failure to recognize reality can derail even the most talented executive. Ask for feedback and take it to heart. A high-EI leader considers feedback a gift and uses it to improve.

To be an extremely effective leader, one needs to become self-aware. Be open to *the experts* (see Chapter 5) and the critics. When you are open to feedback, people around you will challenge you and tell you what you really need to hear. During my career, I heard from the experts and the critics weekly and sometimes daily, publicly. If this doesn't keep you in check, I don't know what will.

EI means knowing yourself and being able to assess others quickly to support better decisions. This is critical for any executive making hundreds of decisions a day. After a day of hundreds of decisions, I didn't want to go home and decide what to have for dinner. The last thing I wanted to do was go home and make more decisions. Can you relate to this? Leaders with strong EI share the burden of decisions and reserve their energies for visionary leadership.

I became self-aware on another level when working with my own executive coach while I was coaching college basketball. It was the best training I ever received; I became a great leader and a more effective coach and leader. It helped me to become better for others around me. That's what it's about: how we as ON POINT leaders affect others positively and negatively. I had to take my leadership to the next level in order for my team and staff to produce consistent results. This awareness changed my life and the people around me; it also became a driving force for choosing my new path to be an executive coach.

SELF-MANAGEMENT

Self-management gives a person the ability to ensure the pot doesn't boil over. A person with high EI also displays high maturity. When reviewing your emotions, make sure you deliver the message and provide motivation the way people need. Everyone receives information and feedback differently. Restraint and control are important in delivering a positive and constructive message.

An emotionally intelligent leader can control his or her moods through self-awareness, change them for the better through self-management, understand their impact through empathy, and act in ways that boost others' moods through relationship management. Those who lack EI find themselves at the mercy of their emotions, constantly battling the challenges that result.

Individuals with high self-management EI have an inner drive, and are often more resilient and optimistic. These are the people you need when there's chaos and the organization is broken. They turn it around. My partner relishes and thrives in chaos—rebuilding and bringing the sunken ship back to the surface. She's done it many times at three different institutions in academics and athletics. She's always been someone who can fix broken cultures; it's amazing watching her do it everywhere she's been. She displays motivation, leadership, high expectations, and accountability consistently.

SOCIAL AWARENESS

The skill of social awareness promotes empathy. Demonstrating compassion, understanding people, and making them feel valued are critical to successful leaders, colleagues, and managers. And, let's not forget about the customer and clients—they need to feel valued and honored. Everyone excels when they feel a sense of empathy from the culture and leadership. They want to know that you care, that you recognize their hard work; they don't want to disappoint you. Being able to navigate your work environment and the politics that exist around your Board, stakeholders, peers, and boss requires social awareness EI, the X-factor that high-level leaders have.

A high-level superior I worked with spent his time at major events in a corner sitting with one person who he was comfortable with. He sat in staff meetings on his cell phone texting and surfing the internet and many times never showed up at the meetings because he thought he was bigger than the meeting itself. This individual had an important position in the organization, yet his behavior indicated a clear lack of leadership, social awareness, and executive presence. He didn't know any better—but everyone else around him knew the score.

We are wired to connect with people but we often sabotage others and ourselves when we don't make the time. People want to feel valued, to know that their voice is heard, and to be acknowledged for their work. The skills to influence others, and the ability to build relationships with people who can make a difference, enable EI and represent what separates the good from the great. Developing strong social awareness EI is a requirement for anyone who is already in a high-level position . . . or you may not have the position for long.

RELATIONSHIP MANAGEMENT

Focus on people skills! Build rapport and trust, avoid drama and backstabbing, and respect and enjoy others. It sounds simple, but for many leaders it's not. These are important qualities that high-performing teams must possess. You need people with high EI who will manage relationships. To meet the needs of people and the demands of a constantly changing environment, traditional management styles don't work anymore. The Millennial generation is skeptical and there are many stagnant workplaces and leaders. People need healthy environments filled with high-EI leaders who will engage, commit to their people, and put a premium on developing and coaching their people and teams.

Most of us operate on autopilot; I did for years. My job was consuming and I spent my days putting out fires, making decisions, and solving problems. It was easier to answer everyone's questions, to make quick decisions for them, and to do things my way rather than listen to their ideas, teach others how to problem solve, and develop better decision makers. Working on your EI skills entails taking a hard look at your strengths and getting off autopilot to be more intentional and purposeful.

We all have blind spots. If we don't know what they are, we will never reach the next level as an ON POINT leader. Marshall Goldsmith, one of the top executive coaches with *Fortune 100* companies, says 70 percent of people think they are in the top 10 percent. This is a major blind spot. Using EI coaching, assessments, 360-degree feedback, and interviews can help you identify where your blind spots are.

Whether it is training or coaching, the focus of EI is to gain more clarity into your strengths and weakness and those of your direct reports and teams. People will trust and connect with you better when you understand their needs. Being authentic and taking time for people will allow you to be a more authentic leader; people can assess authenticity and then decide if they trust someone in a matter of seconds. Developing trust with people and teams will determine whether you are leading successfully or not.

Our responsibility is to develop more leaders in our organization and on our teams. The stronger your relationships, the more effectively you will lead. Knowing others' strengths and providing clarity in what you need from them, you will be more successful getting buy-in. The best leaders empower, have high expectations, and trust their team members. In turn, their team members will run through walls for them. Is this your situation? If not, work on the X-factor. An effective leader leads effectively with EI.

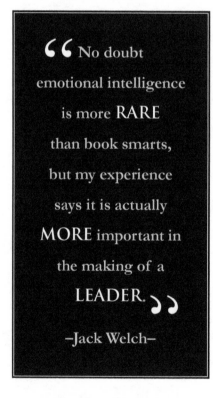

❝ No doubt emotional intelligence is more RARE than book smarts, but my experience says it is actually MORE important in the making of a LEADER. ❞

–Jack Welch–

EI will help you hire better. This is rarely our favorite part of the job. Hiring is hard; finding good people with the right fit is a complex equation. The people you surround yourself with will make or break you. Use EI to assess your team's needs, to evaluate the candidates you hire, and to ease the transition of a new staff member into the existing team.

There is also a dark side of EI. Let's face it, if you have good EI skills, being self-aware, empathetic, and socially conscious can also make you skilled at manipulating others. If you're not cautious, the results could be devastating. EI should be a positive force multiplier—not something that breaks people down at their emotional core.

In total, EI is the backbone of your ability to recognize, understand, and manage your emotions and those of others. If you master EI, you can master the moods and attitudes of yourself and others. Successful leaders demonstrate high EI in corporate America and in big-time college athletics, to the benefit of their peers, teammates, and staff. I could write another book just on this complex, vital topic—it's that important to leadership.

People and their emotional compositions are unique and diverse. Some highly accomplished entrepreneurs, executives, and coaches have little EI. Yet, there is value for every team in fostering EI among all players and team members. The path to achieving meaningful behavioral change is long, arduous, and sometimes painful. Study, invest in, and leverage EI. This ON POINT X-factor will take your leadership to the next level.

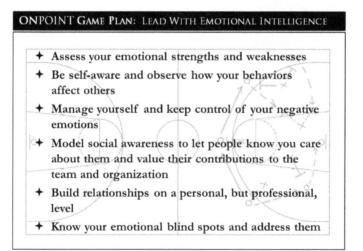

ONPOINT GAME PLAN: LEAD WITH EMOTIONAL INTELLIGENCE

+ Assess your emotional strengths and weaknesses
+ Be self-aware and observe how your behaviors affect others
+ Manage yourself and keep control of your negative emotions
+ Model social awareness to let people know you care about them and value their contributions to the team and organization
+ Build relationships on a personal, but professional, level
+ Know your emotional blind spots and address them

LEARNING FROM FAILED LEADERS

"If you're not making someone else's life better,
you know, you're living your's wrong."
—Will Smith—

We learn more from mistakes and failures, our own and others', more than we learn from successes. Our entire lives we watch and learn from our parents, siblings, coaches, teachers, bosses, peers, and celebrities.

We see what to do and what not to do. We form, mold, develop, and build our own philosophies, management, and leadership styles. We adopt attributes from people we have looked up to and improve on traits from those who failed us as leaders. It's our responsibility to study and to learn from the best, and also the worst, when figuring out who we are and want to be as leaders.

LEARNING LIFE LESSONS

We've all learned from wonderful and inspiring people and situations, but we also learn the most powerful and life-changing lessons about what we would never do. I was a young coach, 22 years old, in my first experience coaching Division I basketball in a very good program and with a very successful head coach. I witnessed great coaching, excellent recruiting, and systemic assembling of a very talented team in a Top 25 program.

I also experienced how people should and should not be treated in front of peers, student-athletes, and others. I witnessed demeaning and humiliation of staff members in front of student-athletes. The players felt badly for the assistants and the assistant coaches were embarrassed. Was this a lack of emotional intelligence, a case of showing others who is the boss, or a situation of just not being aware? As a young but influential coach, I learned I would never treat people like that in front of others, especially impressionable kids. I committed to always respect people—they are busting their butts for me and you. Over time, these poor behaviors wore people down, destroyed respect and trust, and produced a culture where humiliation of others became the norm.

I also learned lessons from another leader who couldn't make a decision. The ability to make thoughtful but timely decisions is critical for leaders. One must be able to make decisions, and good ones, to be respected as a leader. This skill exemplifies the leader's competence and confidence in the decisions they make.

Have you ever been around a boss or peer who couldn't make a decision? The level of frustration this situation creates is significant. These types of leaders and bosses are confusing and uncertain; they will wear you down and question everything you do and everything they did. I worked with a leader like this for many years; it made me feel crazy and undervalued, and it exhausted me and others.

Indecisive leaders can't move a team or organization forward. They are too busy being stuck on an island of uncertainty. Their decisions change daily and they can't make up their minds. They can't decide what they want for lunch or dinner, much less set direction for the team. If this sounds like you or a leader you know, staff has probably changed over frequently and I'm sure you notice their frustration. If you want to retain good staff, decide to stop being indecisive.

Failed leaders also illuminate lessons about cultural fit. Ask yourself, *Does this type of leader fit into my culture and can they bring my organization or team to the next level?* A leader must be the right fit; it is critical to assess a leader's values and connectedness in the context of the organization's climate, expectations, and external factors. In today's business and athletic arenas, establishing leaders who others will follow is the difference between success and failure.

Are you a leader who is known for emotional intelligence, connection with the community, and authenticity and empathy? If so, stand up! You are ON POINT. Unfortunately, there are not many with these necessary qualities packaged with the skill, competitiveness, and drive to get results.

LEARNING TO ENGAGE

Successful leaders seek the sweet spot for engagement and passion. We have all experienced failed leaders who launch into tirades in their management team meetings. Or others who disengage, sitting in a meeting playing on their cell phones or computers and not listening to or respecting the person who is talking. We have all witnessed leaders who belittle people for not having knowledge or performing tasks they consider obvious and routine. It is no wonder why no one speaks up or shares ideas in these leaders' meetings.

I have worked with many high-level leaders who question their teams or staff members when they don't speak up in meetings and don't share their ideas or opinions. Nine times out of ten, this occurs because leaders have shot ideas down, interrupted them or finished their sentences, got defensive, or dismissed ideas. Is this you?

You may not even be aware that your behaviors are shutting others down. The ability to listen and to engage their team members is one of the main areas of improvement for many of my clients. As a matter of fact, I must admit that I once was one of these head coaches and leaders. Over time, I learned more self-awareness and developed better listening skills and patience. I became more open to others' ideas and allowed others to be creative and innovative. I developed the skill of listening more than talking in staff meetings, in team meetings, and with stakeholders. I also delegated staff meeting facilitation to my other staff members so I could just sit and listen.

As I reflect on my career and my future, I have stepped back and assessed my total body of work and how it affects the way I lead, influence, and impact others' lives. What has made me a stronger leader? The ability to cast a greater vision and

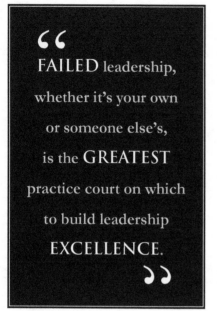

> **FAILED** leadership, whether it's your own or someone else's, is the **GREATEST** practice court on which to build leadership **EXCELLENCE.**

to help others around me achieve more than they ever imagined. The wisdom embedded in my failures and successes allows me to continue moving forward confidently, swiftly, and unstoppably. Understandably, most people would rather not talk about their failures, but they teach us how to manage and to lead through adversity with grace.

FUELED BY FAILURE

Lessons taught from failed leadership shape us as leaders. As both an experienced, elite college basketball coach and now an entrepreneur, mistakes and failure fueled me and provided me with the greatest opportunities to learn in my career. Those difficult times have allowed me to become an expert working with teams and developing leadership. From the people I hired, players I recruited, teams I built, investments I made, decisions I made, relationships in which I invested—in each experience I learned something about leadership and myself. I learned what my players and staff expected of me as their head coach and role model. I learned what donors, people in the community, and parents expected of me as an ON POINT leader. I accepted responsibility because many people counted on me in many different ways. My role and my platform gave me an opportunity to learn, and I embraced it.

The lessons from failed leadership also teach us about survival and reinvention. If you really want to know about another person, see if they have a rudder built through success and failure. Character surfaces if you ask them to talk about their failures; if they can be vulnerable and real with you, coming clean about their failures, then you have found their rudder. Being vulnerable and courageous enough to admit your mistakes, own your failures, take your share of the blame, and accept responsibility are what creates leaders who people will follow.

How you respond and what you do with failure defines your character, illuminates your values, and sets the direction your rudder points to as a leader. Do you admit when you are wrong and do you take responsibility for your team's failures? As an athletics coach, do you take ownership of the defeats? After every mistake or failure I asked myself several questions: *What did I learn from this? What did I learn about the process and the outcome? What would I do differently next time?* When you fail, do you point the finger at someone else, and blame the circumstances that you face, to deflect the criticism of failed results?

In my last season at the University of Minnesota, I had seven healthy players. Each game, I looked down the bench for solutions and was confronted with a lack of bench strength. The entire season, I kept turning and looking and finding only two additional players in uniform. My starting point guard was diagnosed with her third concussion and was out for the reminder of the season. One of my top post players tore her ACL and was out for the second half of the Big Ten season. One of my star freshman players also displayed concussion symptoms and missed much of the season. I could have easily made excuses because of the uncontrollable situation.

In spite of these limitations, I refused to blame the circumstances and our team valiantly fought its way to a 20-win regular season. Great leadership and management require accountability for your responsibilities and the outcomes—good and bad. Some of the greatest coaches, athletic directors, executives, military leaders, and heads of state in history failed or had to overcome overwhelming obstacles. Almost all were fired at one time, or more than once. The ability to find a way through the darkness, to handle failure or firing with grace, and to hold ourselves together has enabled me, and others, to be resilient, to persevere, and to become better leaders. Many successful people have failed as leaders; it's about the lessons we learn from others and ourselves during the process and throughout the journey.

What do successful leaders who learn from failure have in common? We want to be the best at what we do, nothing will stop us, and there is nothing more important in our lives than developing people and understanding people. Being ON POINT as a leader is about becoming better and building our legacies.

My coaching career was filled with a lifetime of laughter, proud moments, proud second mom experiences, and many wins. There were also times where we careened off the rails and traveled down the wrong path—but I don't regret the mistakes and the failures and I never question following my gut. As a veteran leader and as the winningest coach in Minnesota program history, I also experienced drastic changes in leadership styles and a divisive culture with disaster written all over it from day one.

As I navigated the final two years of my career at Minnesota, the price and pain of failed athletic department leadership was deep and wide. The organization and department was rocked. There were many people who may forgive, but they will never forget. Unfortunately, it was apparent that people can be self-serving when they are not used to the spotlight and are unfamiliar with the power their position brings. Power corrupts and is poorly used for personal gain. Leaders can become intoxicated by power, engaging in bad behavior simply because they may feel untouchable. They control and subjugate others. Such leadership for personal desires leads people, teams, and organizations down dark roads.

There are usually smoke signals in each of these situations. People choose to ignore them or they are protecting the people they hired. We discuss organizations as if they're not human, but the moving parts are people—real people with real feelings and families. This situation is more common than we can wrap our heads around, and many organizations systemically allow poor behavior and support it to the detriment of their people, customers, and stakeholders. Eventually, their avoidance and allowance comes home to roost. It does every time; it's just a matter of time. And when it does, the damage is far-reaching and the way out is treacherous.

" Things are NEVER as good or as bad as they seem. "

As an executive coach, I have been fortunate to work with very successful, top-producing leaders. The good ones are easy to spot and fun to work with—their organizations are organically supportive and healthy. As leaders, they are secure with themselves and have deep-rooted values. I can feel it when I walk in the front door. The contrast to leaders who misuse power, abuse control, and fail to take responsibility is as plain as day.

I would not change anything in the lessons I've learned as a leader from my victories and defeats. I wouldn't trade a moment of difficulty or pain. Instead, I've embraced and flourished in every opportunity because I'm determined to be the best. If that means making mistakes and suffering defeats along the way, so be it. This drives me and motivates me to be ON POINT every day.

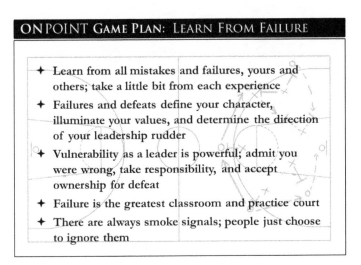

ON POINT GAME PLAN: LEARN FROM FAILURE

+ Learn from all mistakes and failures, yours and others; take a little bit from each experience

+ Failures and defeats define your character, illuminate your values, and determine the direction of your leadership rudder

+ Vulnerability as a leader is powerful; admit you were wrong, take responsibility, and accept ownership for defeat

+ Failure is the greatest classroom and practice court

+ There are always smoke signals; people just choose to ignore them

PART FOUR

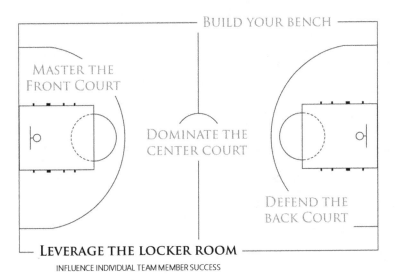

BUILD YOUR BENCH

MASTER THE
FRONT COURT

DOMINATE THE
CENTER COURT

DEFEND THE
BACK COURT

LEVERAGE THE LOCKER ROOM
INFLUENCE INDIVIDUAL TEAM MEMBER SUCCESS

161

SECURING
TEAM BUY-IN

*"The task of leadership is to create an alignment of strengths so strong
that it makes the system's weaknesses irrelevant."*
—Peter Drucker—

**Are you a leader who can't get your team on the same page, moving
in the same direction to accomplish a common goal?** Leadership
requires the capability to translate an inspiring vision into reality. A great
leader needs to start with, and believe in, a compelling vision. Being able
to share and communicate the vision, define roles and responsibilities,
then inspire action are critical to achieve a desired outcome.

ACHIEVING ALIGNMENT

I have a client, Ryan, who is the project manager of the biggest, most expensive, and highest-visibility projects in his organization. Ryan leads a large
team inside and outside of the organization in this project. Over the course
of the next two years, the project will replace a system that has existed for decades. Ryan can't fail; the new system must be implemented successfully in the
next two years.

Sounds like a tough assignment, but what's the real challenge? The project is not
about Ryan, it's about getting his team to buy into the vision and their roles, then

enabling all team members to move in the same direction and execute this project on the biggest stage. Teamwork is crucial in accomplishing the largest project this organization has experienced in decades.

Ryan's greatest challenge is that his team is not aligned and, consequently, they are struggling to implement the system. Accomplishing this project will take teamwork, great chemistry, and everyone following and executing the leader's vision. Many leaders are unsuccessful in building functional teams. In many business situations, team members are confused in defining team objectives, establishing roles and responsibilities, getting the right people in the right positions and setting project goals. To accomplish any goal, a leader must create a culture that supports healthy dialogue and collaboration in order to get alignment in these areas.

Team leaders must provide clear expectations for individuals and the team. Proper planning, building basic fundamentals, and laying a solid foundation is where one must start as a leader. Creating concise goals, clarifying roles, setting a vision, and communicating pose difficulties for most teams—these are crucial skills and attributes successful teams embrace.

As a leader, I have always started with the individual. Individual growth leads to team growth, which produces organizational growth. Each component of your environment must be healthy; it's a constant work in progress. Make sure you manage your team and motivate them as individuals. This will allow them to play to their strengths and be contributing members to the team. Their involvement and commitment to collaboration leads to one of a team's greatest success factors: buy-in!

You can't lead the same way you did a decade ago. If you are, you may be frustrated and underperforming. Great leadership today is authentic and making sure everyone understands the "Why," individually and as a team. What is your "Why"? Know your ultimate purpose, then share it and learn what makes your team members tick. My "Why" and purpose is to develop more efficient and effective leaders, and to help them navigate the challenges they face on a daily basis.

One of a leader's greatest responsibilities is developing and mentoring. Consider it a golden opportunity to develop those who are following. Accept these responsibilities as your obligation to the individual, the team, and the organization. Look around—in front, behind, and across; who is next in line for a leadership position? Are you developing sustainability in your own team and in the organization? Fulfilling the responsibility to develop, mentor, and promote from within is one of a leader's most rewarding experiences.

Growing up and navigating home, school, and athletics, I didn't have many mentors. There were few women in leadership positions I could look to for guidance, advice, and support. As I matured and understood the gaps I experienced, I decided to do what others said I couldn't do: become an influential leader. It fueled my fire that I was running against popular wisdom. I was going to change the mindset. In your life you have probably experienced something similar and, like me, when you are under duress, your true character comes out. Don't be afraid to challenge yourself.

We know from research that the best teams and most efficient organizations operate successfully because they are aligned and have diverse teams. It's classic Myers Briggs personality assessment in action. Take the assessment then pair yourself with someone who's on the opposite end of the spectrum. These are some of the most interesting combinations, where seemingly conflicting attributes may generate creativity and innovation.

Women bring a special skillset to business and the community. We all need this dynamic on our teams. However, women generally lack confidence and typically are not comfortable taking risks. Men tend to feel that they can do more and they can do it better. If your team operates with only the traditional male psyche and lacks a fe-

> " A critical aspect in getting buy-in is to build a **DIVERSE** team. Diverse teams operate **BETTER** at the next level. "

male perspective, imagine what you are missing. Could the intuitive and collaborative skills of a woman make a difference? What if you had a balanced dialogue for critical decisions that need to be made? I know that's what I, and other progressive leaders, prefer! Bring women to the table. They have collaborative strengths and bring emotional intelligence to problem-solving and decision-making.

Once you get buy-in, a balanced team in place, and everyone in the right roles, then it's time to instill confidence in each of them individually and as a team. To achieve buy-in and to engender support in you as a leader, focus energy on building meaningful relationships and demonstrating that you value your people. This is the secret to long-term retention and loyalty. And, it is an opportunity to strengthen your understanding of basic human behavior and emotional intelligence.

When you establish buy-in and confidence in your individuals and your team, they will feel valued and powerful in what they bring to the team and organization. Pointing out strengths, complimenting an employee, and creating a vision seem simple—but it's not. Communicating an inspiring vision and getting buy-in and your team aligned are skills that great leaders have, but also many leaders lack.

Let's start with you. Are you successful as a leader in creating a vision for yourself, your team, and the organization? Are you able to build a team, get buy-in, and get your team to follow you as the leader in accomplishing a common goal?

For women, a lack of confidence often stands as their greatest barrier to success. Women are remarkably strong individuals who have the capability to battle adversity and to conquer challenges, but their own self-confidence and self-doubt bring them down more times than not. Women tend to focus on negative instead of positive self-talk. Their internal conversations lean toward second-guessing their actions, dissecting their appearance, and questioning their self-worth no matter how successful or powerful they seem to be. This negative self-talk gets so loud it can bring one down to their knees. It's difficult for a woman to project executive presence and share her vision when she's struggling internally with herself.

Greatness comes from having confidence. Confidence comes from being extremely prepared, building routines, and practicing. People have powerful memories of being part of a team, the camaraderie in accomplishing a common goal, and achieving a successful end result. The leader who can build that confidence and gain buy-in from their teams in the vision is unstoppable.

CULTIVATING TEAM DYNAMICS

So, you're in a leadership role and you have a team. Let's discuss team dynamics. I have found many leaders struggle to give praise and positive reinforcement. Why? It's the simplest thing to do. Like many leaders, my expectations run high, too. For many of the leaders I coach and consult, one of the top three areas of improvement is to provide more encouragement, positive reinforcement, and praise. Sometimes, leaders deny that this is their role or responsibility because there's a sense that, *It's their job, why do I need to tell them how well they're doing? It's expected. They're being soft.* If this is the mindset we have as leaders, it will be difficult to get buy-in and to draw the most out of your team.

The ideal praise-to-constructive-criticism ratio is 5 to 1, according to 2004 research by Emily Heaphy and Marcial Losada. Are you mindful of this ratio as you interact with people? Look around and observe your team members; are they happy, do they feel valued, and is your team heading in the same direction? If not, your self-awareness is low and the problem might be you.

> " ENGAGE the individuals on your team, and PRAISE and ENCOURAGE them on a daily basis, and you will instill CONFIDENCE and CONSISTENTLY get buy-in. "

First and foremost, all leaders must take steps to build trust, confidence, loyalty, and goodwill among their teams. This will lead the organization on a path of sustainable success. If your people feel appreciated and respected, and buy in to you and your vision, they will care about the success of the organization. For overall growth and sustainability of the organization, it is important to value your people and build confidence—this is your role as an ON POINT leader.

One of my former players, a walk-on, is a perfect example of getting an individual to buy in to a vision, role, and a common goal no matter what their status on the team. After enrolling as a freshman (before she was on the team), she attended every home game and sat up in the nosebleed section with her father. She sat there because it was the only seat left in the arena with over 14,000 in attendance.

After the season, she came to my office and asked if she could try out and walk on to the team the following season. I told her that we were not sure if we were taking walk-ons and couldn't commit to holding tryouts in the fall. I asked her to stop back later. And she did—she stopped back a week later. And then a week after that. She was persistent. She really wanted to be part of the team. She was going to do whatever it took to be part of a women's basketball team that had just experienced its first-ever Sweet 16.

Finally I laid out the deal for her. I gave her a worst-case scenario on what she could possibly expect in her role on the team. I said, *You will most likely never play a minute in a game, may never get on the floor, and possibly may not even practice. I hoped that she could prove me wrong.* I continued, *If you can could handle these conditions, you can be on the team.* She shook my hand and replied with certainty, *I won't disappoint you, I'm going to work my tail off and I'm looking forward to proving you wrong.* She left my office and for her sophomore and junior years, she paid her own way to college, she never saw the floor unless we were up by 40 points, and she became a fan favorite.

She bought into the team's overall goals, the program vision, and her role. She was the one at the end of the bench waving the towel getting the fans into the game. She was the first one on her feet to meet the team heading to the bench for a timeout. She was the first one who would give encouragement to her teammates and the coaching staff. Despite the challenges of her role, she became irreplaceable.

The start of her senior year, I rewarded her by putting her on a full scholarship. She was as valuable as the star of the team, yet in two years had barely had an impact during a game. Her senior year, she accepted and bought into one of the most difficult roles on the team. Her role, in practices, was to guard the best point guard in the country—one of the best women's basketball players ever to play the game. And what happened? She came out swinging. She embraced the challenge and dogged her opponent up and down the court. It brought out her best and raised the game of the player she guarded, who would go on to a successful career in the WNBA and win a gold medal in the Olympics.

She played in the closing minutes of 16 games that season, securing her spot as a fan favorite because of her buy-in for her team and teammates. Our booster club created an award modeled after her: she received the inaugural "For the Love of the Game" award at our annual team banquet that year. Her determination became the storyline to one of the most memorable experiences, players, and life lessons of my coaching career. I am the one who learned from her and am grateful for the opportunity. She followed her passion and is now a very successful mother, wife, and businesswoman who is doing what she truly believes in.

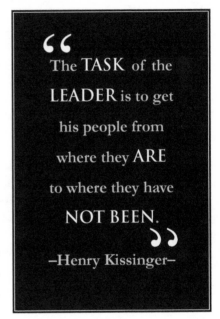

" The **TASK** of the **LEADER** is to get his people from where they **ARE** to where they have **NOT BEEN.** "

–Henry Kissinger–

She was instrumental that season in supporting an inspiring vision for the team. Gaining buy-in, with the team aligned and heading in the same direction, was a critical step on the road to the Final Four.

Instilling confidence in your people and teams will provide a healthier culture, enable greater retention, and contribute to a more profitable bottom line. ON POINT leaders emphasize teamwork by getting individuals to focus on team-oriented goals, making everyone feel important and valued no matter what their role. Without everyone's buy-in, your project, your team, and your organization won't reach full potential.

ON POINT GAME PLAN: SECURE BUY-IN

+ Share and communicate an inspiring vision
+ Identify and leverage the strengths of each one of your team members
+ Communicate effectively to achieve buy-in on roles and responsibilities with each person on the team
+ Establish a culture with healthy dialogue and collaboration
+ Set goals together as a team
+ Build a diverse and balanced team with different strengths and perspectives, yet with a common goal
+ Build confidence in your people

THE POWER OF
POSITIVITY

*"The greatest discovery of all time is that a person can change
his future by merely changing his attitude."*
—Oprah Winfrey—

**I am a believer in the power of positivity and the connectedness
that results from it.** You know the saying: *people do business with people they
trust and like.* It applies to more than sales and business. We all want to
surround ourselves with positive people. What type of person comprises
your inner circle? Do you lift others up or do you bring others down?

START WITH BELIEF

It doesn't start with positivity toward others; it starts with being positive
toward yourself. When was the last time you said, *I believe in me?* I believe in
myself and I always have. It doesn't mean that I'm arrogant or cocky or have
a big head. It means that I have a strong belief in my values and self-confidence. I
know my capabilities and believe I will succeed.

Belief is actually my top strength in the Strengths Finder 2.0. I value responsibility and high ethics—in others and in myself. My core values affect my behavior
in many ways. They give my life meaning and satisfaction; my belief in success
represents more than a drive for money and prestige.

My values provide direction and guidance through the distractions that life presents. My values and belief are the foundation of my relationships. My friends see me as dependable and they always know where I stand. Belief also makes one easy to trust. I have always aligned my values with my work. Work must be meaningful; it all matters to me. Belief has allowed me to live out my values in all that I do.

There isn't a more powerful tool and strength that an ON POINT leader and coach can use than positivity. The endless opportunities we all have to impact other's lives and to make a difference in a positive way is the biggest rush anyone could ever have. This is life-changing for the person giving and receiving positivity.

I believe in you. When was the last time you heard these words? How many times have you heard these words from your boss, co-workers, friends, or family? These are potent, influential words that can change someone's day and transform their lives.

Try it the next time you walk into you place of employment and you tell one of your co-workers or your boss, *I believe in you.* These words were powerful with my players; face-to-face or in a simple text message, the power of positivity is like no other. When is the last time you said, *I believe in you,* to your son or daughter? If it was recent, great job! Do it again. If you can't remember the last time you told your own kids that you believe in them, try it today. You will lift them up and you will see the look in their eyes, the smile on their face, and the attitude that you believe in them—it is so powerful.

> **LOOKING** into someone's eyes **CHANGES** the entire conversation. "

I had a player in my last four years of coaching at Minnesota who was trying to find herself, to like herself, and to believe in herself. She was experiencing an eating disorder, was in an abusive relationship, lost her starting position, and was thousands of miles away from home. To see her like this just tore me up. I was her mentor, role model, and second mom.

One day I was sitting with her talking after practice and as I looked into her eyes, I said, *I believe in you more than you will ever know.* She broke down into tears and just cried. I held her closely and we shared a special moment. To this day, I take so much pride in the relationship I have with her. The power of those words was magical and created a memorable moment for both of us.

It doesn't take much effort to say these simple words to a few people each day. Build someone up. Remind them that they're valued. Tell them they are special. Be the light in a life that may seem dim at times. *I believe in you.*

RECOGNIZE VALUE AND CONTRIBUTION

One of my client's goals is to provide more positive feedback and encouragement to employees, peers, and stakeholders. In learning to increase emotional intelligence, an exercise I often use requires a client to track every time they give a compliment, provide encouragement, and use words of positivity throughout the day. I also have them keep track of the times they missed an opportunity. I have them do this for a week.

This exercise with high-level leaders is powerful. They increase their self-awareness on how they make people feel, how they lift others up, and how much it actually increases their own happiness in the workplace. Producing even greater impact, they become increasingly self-aware of the missed opportunities. Armed with this evidence and newfound awareness, my clients can create positive change in their behavior and improve the effects their words have on others.

This is a crucial step in enabling high-performing people and building teams. Who doesn't need compliments, to be told that they are doing a great job, to hear *please* and *thank you,* and to feel appreciation for hard work for the organization? When this happens, notice how it makes you feel and how it impacts the person you addressed. For a high-level ON POINT leader, this is a best practice in being effective. Part of executing vision, goals, and expectations is executing the game plan. Within this a leader needs to provide momentum.

People perform at the level that's expected. Are you a driven and proactive leader? This creates a positive environment. Do you provide feedback and offer praise? This creates a culture of gratitude, happiness, retention, good health, positive feelings, and a more profitable bottom line. Why don't people do this more often? It's one of the top actions that high-level leaders need to understand and to employ more often. It's not that hard to say something positive to your people and teams that work so hard for you and your organization on a daily basis.

It's amazing that giving a compliment and using simple words of encouragement can have such a significant and powerful impact. Tears might well up and, you can be sure, broad smiles and deep pride will shine. These are best practices that we all, and especially the ON POINT leader, should use every day. As you start your day, I challenge you to speak these four words—*I believe in you*—more often to your spouse, children, and co-workers. The more you give, the more you will receive.

ONPOINT GAME PLAN: LEAD WITH POSITIVITY

+ Believe in yourself first
+ Believe in others; it's powerful and transformative
+ Be self-aware of how you are impacting others with your words
+ Keep track of each time you use the power of positivity and of each missed opportunity for a week
+ Communicate to others that you believe in them through words of encouragement, compliments, and recognition

LEADING A MULTIGENERATIONAL WORKPLACE

"We should invest in people, not ideas. A good idea is often destroyed by bad people and good people can always make a bad idea better."
—Simon Sinek—

Coaching, developing, and mentoring are arguably the most powerful methods for increasing leadership capabilities in your people. The young employees of today are the future business leaders of tomorrow. As leaders, we have an obligation to cultivate a more robust future by training and mentoring tomorrow's leaders today. How do we develop and keep the best young talent in an organization?

The impact leaders have on their people and teams transforms organizations and changes lives. Great leaders accept and relish the opportunity to develop team members and to coach others, recognizing the powerful benefit for their team members and the organization. Many leaders undervalue or disregard their responsibility to coach people. This is a missed opportunity, and yes, it is one of the leader's greatest responsibilities.

Leaders in executive positions struggle to balance the varying demands at work and in their lives. Typically they multi-task and spend many years moving at a sprinter's pace. The resulting intensity and stress are so high that the last thing a leader may think about is coaching and developing their people.

THE LEADER AS COACH

W ho wouldn't want to be a coach? Have you ever been called Coach? For those who have never been a coach, it feels inspiring and intoxicating to experience the coach's role. Many people dream of being a coach: it's a role that embodies the respect, admiration, influence, and impact that one can have on people's lives. Who doesn't want that?

I have been Coach as long as I can remember and today as an executive coach, everyone still calls me Coach. Once you're a coach, you're always a coach. When you're in a leadership position, one of the most important roles you have is to develop leaders. Here are a few reasons why leaders need to find the time and create space to be a coach and to develop leadership:

❖ Partnering and collaboration are rewarding and engender loyalty

❖ Shared responsibility means less that the leader has to do alone

❖ Coaching evokes people's creativity and talent for their benefit and the value of the organization

❖ People become less dependent on the leader for direction, and that frees the leader up for visionary thinking and strategic action

❖ The leader's scope of influence can be much broader when the leader doesn't have to micromanage their people

❖ The leader has more time to develop new areas of expertise that will add value to the organization and further his/her career

In a recent worldwide survey of nearly 500 CEOs carried out by management consulting firm McKinsey & Company, 83 percent of executives felt that leadership development was one of the top three current and future priorities in their organizations. This sounds progressive and even positive, yet only 7 percent felt that their organizations currently were effective in developing a qualified leadership pipeline to address their organizational focus.

Successful executives recognize that building their organization's high potentials and their future leaders is a major differentiator and enables orderly succession for the organization. A leadership pipeline in your organization should be a top priority. If you're not doing it, your competitors may be—and they may steal your best talent.

Progressive executive leaders realize they must venture into new waters for behaviors, concepts, processes, and best practices to enable their people to develop the qualities necessary for success today and in the future. The CEO owns the ultimate responsibility for this focused effort and his or her philosophies and actions must truly reflect the importance of leadership development.

MODERN-DAY LEADERSHIP

My battle cry to executive leaders is to develop into modern-day leaders. There is nothing more important than building relationships with your peers, bosses, and direct reports. To connect and engage, it is more important now than ever to get out of your office and walk down the hallway to listen to and to talk with your people. Ask questions, get to know your team, and be present in the moment.

Leading in today's four-generation workforce environment presents a challenging terrain to navigate for executive leaders. People in the workforce are living longer so they are working later in their years. The Millennial generation makes up the largest portion of our workforce today, and is one of the most difficult generations to understand and to embrace for an older, more experienced senior-level executive.

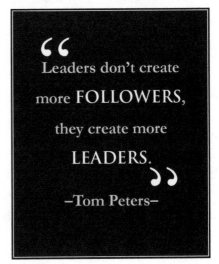

66
Leaders don't create

more FOLLOWERS,

they create more

LEADERS.
"

–Tom Peters–

Senior leaders should coach and mentor these young employees to drive the success of their organizations. Young people graduate from academic institutions armed with academic knowledge, enthusiasm, and idealism. Then, they quickly realize that they lack the skills required to navigate and to succeed in a corporate environment. When employees of different generations work together on projects, more experienced staff can impart knowledge and lessons to less experienced team members. However, the potential also may arise for an unhealthy rivalry and a contentious relationship. The young employee may feel the mature employee is stuck in their ways and unwilling to explore alternatives, and the veteran employee may see youthful exuberance as undisciplined, unrealistic, or threatening.

Many businesses are implementing reverse mentoring—where not just the more experienced serve as mentors, but the younger generation also mentors their more experienced counterparts. Both groups have completely different, and valuable, skillsets and talents. I spoke to a group of seniors in college at a Leaders of the Future conference on the east coast. One of the engineering students approached me after the conference and asked me for some advice. She said, *I am doing an internship at a large firm and I am working with a lot of older, veteran, and more experienced people who have been at this company for decades. How do I help motivate people who have been at this company for over 20 years when it seems like the only reason they are there is to get a paycheck?* She also asked, *What are we supposed to do if no one will listen to our ideas?* There were more questions . . . but I will save those for another time. Her questions frame the issue: the Millennial generation wants to contribute and worries about how they will do so.

Everyone in your organization—top down, bottom up, and across—should be a part of the process to drive growth and innovation. Whether a star or a role player, an employee has the pulse of the process and knows what actually needs to be done. If the leader can make everyone feel like they are part of the process, the results will speak for themselves.

While coaching a client CEO, I met with the company's leadership team. After two hours, the team felt empowered, listened to, and was able to create solutions and solve problems collaboratively. They respected their boss and felt like they were fortunate to work for one of the best CEOs they had ever experienced. A tremendous amount was accomplished and, heading into a new year with lofty goals, the team was positioned to achieve higher performance.

In business, as in life, there's nothing more certain than change. Whether you like it or not, you must manage in a fast-paced environment, problem-solving rapidly and making split-second decisions. This level of managing change can generate fear or exhilaration—it's your choice how you perceive and address it. In any event, you can count on the world continuing to operate on a larger scale, on a faster platform, and with bolder intentions.

As a leader, do you have the ability to influence others to follow you? Are you a leader who can bring people together and continually monitor and realign as conditions and needs change? Are you setting the stage to propose a plan for effective implementation? When you build relationships to influence and to leverage personal power, people will be drawn to YOU and your vision.

> " Personal power is a source of INFLUENCE one has over their people and teams. Follow this FORMULA: relationships equal influence, influence equals personal power, the essence of your SUCCESS is personal power. "

Athletic coaches take a group of individuals and motivate them to perform and to excel in high-pressure, high-speed, and time-constrained situations every day. What parallels can we make to business? Just like athletics, business involves speed, managing change, and decision-making under pressure. Achieving high performance in business and athletics requires a successful approach to these dynamic conditions.

From decades of coaching teams and elite athletes, I want to share six core values I currently use with my clients. For each one I have listed questions for you to consider. The objective is to introduce conscious and conscientious thought around these concepts. Reflect on each one of the core values—your success as an ON POINT leader depends on it.

1. *Personal Power:* As a leader, do you have the personal power to influence and to develop others? Who is jumping in your boat and following your vision and passion? Look around. Who is following? Who is hanging back . . . and why?

2. *Achievement:* What are your goals, results, and accomplishments? How do you measure success? What are your "wins"—in the workplace and in your life? Do you consider yourself a coach, role model, and mentor? If not, why not?

3. *Intimacy:* Emotional intelligence includes a leader's ability to develop and manage meaningful relationships. What is your communication style? Are you an open and genuine leader? How do you build trust with your board, staff, employees, and stakeholders? Are you willing to share your hopes, dreams, and fears? Be a coach who inspires and teaches others.

4. *Creativity and Innovation:* What gives you energy during the day? Do those around you have the space and time to be creative? How do you express your creativity? What does your workday look like? How much time do you invest in training, coaching, and developing others? This should be one of your professional legacy goals.

5. *Search for Meaning:* What is your purpose and are you looking for more meaning in your life? What does a meaningful life look like? Clarify your values, align your strengths with those values, and develop a vision and purpose around your framework. Are you instilling these values in the people and teams around you?

6. *Compassion and Contribution:* What will your legacy be and what mark will you leave in this world? How do you connect with people and stoke

their energy and passions? One of the most important roles of an ON POINT leader is to motivate, coach, and develop their people and teams.

Successful leaders constantly looking for ways to improve in order to be more effective. You can improve by taking more time to coach and to develop your own people. Personal power, the essence of your success, is learned through experience by building relationships and nurturing a robust support structure. Look at these core values or develop your own, focus on them, and take your leadership game to the next level.

THE MULTIGENERATIONAL WORKPLACE

A hot topic (as discussed in Chapter 7) is recruiting, motivating, and retaining top talent. Within this space, motivating and leading Millennials in the workplace has surfaced as the (multi)million-dollar question. However, the solution doesn't address a single generation, it's about motivating across multiple generations and understanding that you can't motivate and manage everyone in the same manner. As a leader, it is your responsibility to know how to coach the different generations you have on your team and to train each individual according to his or her needs.

We all have Traditionalists, Boomers, Generation X, and Millennials in our workplace—and we are lucky to have all of these generations on a team. It's a great opportunity to learn how to motivate across generations and to leverage the different skillsets these generations offer. If you engage and motivate each team member in the same fashion, you're not considering their individuality and you're probably not being effective.

In college athletics, I coached, led, and mentored young, inexperienced contributors for decades. Considering the rise and role of the Millennial generation in our workforce, today's leaders must be visionary and mindful of their unique perspectives, and skillful in combining different work styles and experiences across multiple generations. The Millennial generation typically is more skilled with technology and social media use, and they bring a much more dynamic skillset for information processing and decision-making. And, they want to work more collaboratively.

One of the most rewarding aspects I've found in developing and coaching Millennials on and off the court has been watching them arrive as "knuckleheads" and, four or five years later when they graduate, sending them into the world as strong, confident, battle-tested young adults. Over the course of my tenure, working with Millennials was frustrating and stressful—but was also rewarding and enlightening. I had to learn how to embrace them quickly because my job depended on the high performance of these 18- to 22-year-olds. I learned as much (or more) from them as they learned from me.

It took me a while to get it. It really did. I thought this generation was spoiled; it seemed they had all the answers and that their parents did everything for them. While some of this reputation for the Millennial generation is warranted, I was tasked with enabling them to perform at a very high level as individuals and as a team. Quickly, I had to overcome my generalizations and to find the recipe to coach them effectively.

What I did learn was to engage and to embrace each of them, as individuals. I took time to learn about them as people: how they communicated, how they worked best, what they cared about, and what music they liked (I even learned what emojis were all about!). After engaging each one, I figured out the approach. They needed connectedness—to feel valued, to be listened to, to be involved, to collaborate, and so much more.

Leaders in business often are frustrated with the Millennial generation. If you refuse to embrace them and to meet them where they are, you will continue to be ineffective. They are almost half of the workforce today and their role and prevalence are only growing. Today, Millennials comprise 36 percent of the workforce. In a few years, it will be 50 percent and then 75 percent in less than a decade. You really don't have a choice, so embrace them and you'll learn a lot. If you do, the reverse mentoring and learning you receive might enrich your career and pave the way to greater success.

We all have teams comprising various generations. When I was coaching athletics, the ages of my staff looked like this: 62, 57, 51, 40, 35, 27, 26, 25, and 24. I was leading, managing, and motivating across generations. Did I motivate and manage them all the same? Absolutely not. Everyone has different preferences and tendencies in the workplace. The more agile you are as a leader, the more effective you will be.

Historically, athletic coaches (often like executive leaders) have Type-A personalities: high-strung, stubborn, and aggressive with a tendency to believe "it's my way or the highway." The traditional executive leader also reflects this style. What once was the favored approach to high performance is now dead on arrival. A new leadership style is required to meet the demands of today and to realize the potential of tomorrow.

As an ON POINT leader, I evolved my leadership style over the course of three decades. I learned to compromise, collaborate, and listen. I've become mindful of those I add to my team and engage in my life. I challenge you to expand your perspective and to build your skills to lead every individual to meet their needs, not yours. If you do, look forward to remarkable rewards for you and your team and sustainable results for your organization.

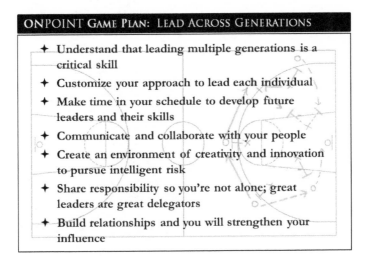

ONPOINT GAME PLAN: LEAD ACROSS GENERATIONS

+ Understand that leading multiple generations is a critical skill
+ Customize your approach to lead each individual
+ Make time in your schedule to develop future leaders and their skills
+ Communicate and collaborate with your people
+ Create an environment of creativity and innovation to pursue intelligent risk
+ Share responsibility so you're not alone; great leaders are great delegators
+ Build relationships and you will strengthen your influence

PRODUCING STRONG DAUGHTERS

"At the end of the day, the most overwhelming key to a child's success is the positive involvement of parents."
–Jane D. Hull–

I don't have a daughter or any children of my own, but every year of my coaching career I had 15 young women on my teams as my daughters. Parents would bring their daughters to me as a surrogate, whether they lived minutes away from campus, across the country, or on another continent.

She's all yours, Coach. We trust that over the next four years our daughter will become a better person, graduate from college, and reach her potential on and off the court. There is no one we would rather have than you. This was the highest compliment I could ever receive from a parent, entrusting me with their child's life and development after leaving their home of 18 years. I was the next adult in their lives to influence their development, serving as coach, mentor, and mother figure for some of the most challenging years of their lives. What a great responsibility and an honor it was to fulfill that expectation in my work at Bowling Green State University, Boston College, and the Universities of Vermont and Minnesota.

Some young women arrived better prepared to tackle the rigors of college life and athletics. Being a student-athlete in major-college athletics is more difficult that most can ever imagine. Each of their worlds were rocked in every way you could imagine. Nothing ever prepares an 18-year-old for college and the emotional, mental, and physical expectations of playing major-college athletics.

HELICOPTER PARENTS

My first task as a collegiate coach began in the recruiting process, but not with the players—with their parents. I had to communicate with, advise, listen to, and challenge the parents to break their own molds. Each young woman's final year in high school was an important opportunity to prepare and to ready them for what they would face in college. Some parents were open to my counsel and others still needed to have control, to protect, to coddle, and to cling to their helicopter parent role and rules. These parents hovered over their daughters and swooped in to rescue them at the first sign of trouble or if something didn't go their way. As college recruiters and coaches, we could spot helicopter parents a mile away and within just minutes of speaking to them.

Coaches have special radar for parents and kids who fit this profile. Unfortunately, it is common for parents today to be overly involved. Generational, societal, and economic factors contribute to an environment of excessive parenting, such as Millennial behavioral tendencies, the rise of hyper-competitive youth sports and training, higher education costs, and social media and informational over-exposure. Parents, if you fit the helicopter profile, everyone around you knows. I have sat in bleachers, stood on sidelines, visited hundreds of high schools, have taken many phone calls, and have watched and spoken to thousands of parents. I have passed on talented players because of their parents. The story in Chapter 23 about a player's parents screaming at her from the stands during a game is one of many cases I witnessed first-hand.

From my coach's perspective, the parent's job is to support, encourage, and serve as a role model for your kids. If I could give you any advice to be more effective and to help your kids, I would recommend that you learn how to communicate with them, teach them how to be resilient and not to quit when facing adversity, and teach them how to have hard conversations. Are you having a tough time having your own hard conversations with your son or daughter? Are you struggling to communicate effectively with your own kids? And, when things get hard, are you allowing them to quit and not finish what they started? These are crucial life skills.

Many student-athletes I've coached did not arrive with these skills in their freshman year. Some did, and that is great parenting. These young adults had an easier time adjusting to the challenges of college life, relating to their coaches and their professors, being away from home, and coping with the pressures and expectations of college athletics. These were the players who played immediately and we considered "no-maintenance" players.

Resiliency was a priority when we recruited student-athletes. We made sure they wouldn't quit if challenges got too hard or if things didn't go their way. If the support wasn't strong enough at home, we would not offer them a scholarship. We couldn't take chances. We communicated to every parent that they couldn't bail their daughter out and allow them to quit every time they would call home expressing frustration or difficulty. We told them to expect these phone calls, to understand that we needed their support, and to know that it was all part of the process to develop strong, resilient, confident, battle-tested young adults. When (not if) they call, just listen, encourage, support, and tell them to talk to the coaches.

There are hundreds of stories, examples, successes, and missteps I have experienced working with parents and their kids. I will share a few success stories and advice I gave a few of my players' parents over the years. I'm not guaranteeing that these lessons work for everyone, but they worked for these individuals.

I received a verbal commitment from a highly touted, nationally recognized player. The summer before she started her senior year of high school, the player's mother called me on the phone. She was concerned about her daughter being so far away from home and questioned her ability to make smart decisions at college, such as staying out too late at night. I wondered to myself, *How would her daughter transition to college and not act like she just was let out of a cage?* After she communicated her concerns, I paused and asked her, *Do you trust your daughter?* She said, *Absolutely.* I replied, *Then why don't you eliminate her curfew?*

She pushed and battled over the phone for 30 minutes and we had a great conversation. We challenged each other and she was uncomfortable in eliminating the curfew. Before we hung up, she said, *I need to really think about this Coach, but I will give it serious thought.* Three months later she called me out of the blue and said, *Thank you, you were right.* I said, *What are you talking about?* The mother continued, *As soon as we had the conversation about eliminating my daughter's curfew, I did.* Anxiously, I asked, *What happened?* She explained that her daughter had been without a curfew for three months and there had been no issues at all. Her parents allowed her to make her own decisions, to come and go as she pleased, and she had been very respectful and trustworthy. In fact, the mother reported that her daughter had been home most nights earlier than before with the curfew. I was amazed and pleased. Finally, she said, *Coach. I thought you were nuts and wondered what you were trying to do to us as parents.* I laughed and responded, *I'm really just trying to make things easier for me when she comes here!*

The more structure, life skills, and freedom to learn that parents provide, the more self-sufficient and successful the kids will be when they branch out on their own. They need certain skills or they will struggle in more ways than you know. Then you will ask yourself, *What happened? What did I do wrong?* Or, you may believe it is someone else's fault.

BACK TO BASICS

As a coach, there are many skills and lessons my staff and I taught our student-athletes because many came without these skills. Many of these are basic, fundamental expectations of respectful, well-mannered human beings. Please support expectations like these and teach your kids—they will thank you someday.

1. *We taught them how to shop for groceries.* Most of them did not know how to shop for healthy food and to buy groceries for themselves. This was done for them their entire lives.

2. *I know you will be shocked, but we taught them to clean up after themselves.* They left garbage lying around, jammed their lockers full, and turned the

locker room upside down like a hurricane swept through. I believed that was very disrespectful and that they should treat the facilities like their home. Unfortunately, I think they did just that. Of course, our expectations required them to pick up after themselves.

3. *We expected them to say please and thank you.* These expressions convey respect. Yes, it's the simple things.

4. *We taught them how to send a thank you note to someone who donated money, bought a season ticket, or sent flowers.* Appreciating others is a building block for leadership.

5. *We taught them how to respect guests and authority.* Before becoming a leader, it helps if you first learn to follow.

6. *We taught them how to properly greet people when someone entered the room.* Recognizing others and putting aside our own ego-centric tendencies demonstrate humility.

7. *We also expected our student-athletes to put their cell phones away at the dinner table when they were having meals with each other.* This was the time to get to know their teammates, to learn about their interests and their families, and to listen to their successes and struggles. It was important to learn how to have a conversation around a dinner table—to be able to engage and laugh with, learn about, and love their sisters.

I could share many more lessons we taught; my players would say that it was a daily "learn fest" in and around the team. In the end, we taught our young women to be ON POINT, to be confident, and to lead themselves and others. We taught them how to walk into a room, navigate airport terminals, and walk into an arena ready to compete with confidence and courage. We showed them how to walk onto the court towards the center circle and shake the opposition's hand, with a confident aura, ready to go to battle. They carried themselves with the leadership presence of strong, confident, and prepared young women. We were their coaches, mentors, and role models—we accepted the responsibility and set the expectation.

MENTORS FOR LIFE

Women need other women. We often have friends and family to rely on, but there are not enough women mentors or women in leadership roles to support young women professionally. Who are the strong female role models your daughter has in her life, other than her mother? There are not enough mentors and, in some cases, women actually work against each other. Unfortunately, it is not uncommon that female executives don't deal well with the success of female subordinates or high-potential females inside or outside their organization. Women need to lift other women up instead of tearing them down.

A mentor relationship is great if you can find a woman-to-woman mentorship. We should not assume that a mentor relationship is the same for a woman as it is for a man. Men and women are different professionally, socially, and emotionally and they tend to need different things. However, I've had as many male mentors as female and they all have been wonderful relationships; it's a great idea for a young woman to have both. And, in all likelihood, because everyone's going to be at different stages of development, the more diversity the better.

Mom and dad need to be role models and mentors for their daughters. Support, encourage, and learn how to talk to and communicate with them. Not on a peer-to-peer level, not as their best friend, but as a parent to your child. This does not mean you should fight their battles, speak for them, and live your lives through them. Prepare them for the challenges, hard knocks, and unforeseen battles they will face on a daily basis.

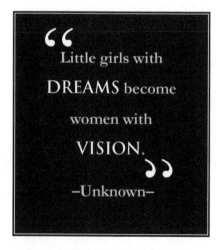

> " Little girls with **DREAMS** become women with **VISION.** "
> —Unknown—

Encourage your daughters to own and to realize their strengths. They have many. Are your daughters able to communicate or write down their strengths and the things they like about themselves? Recognize their strengths and validate their self-worth. Foster their confidence when they're facing adversity or going through change. Encourage and expect them to dream big. Your daughter can be anything she wants.

In Chapter 10, I write about being a driven and caring coach. Be a driven and caring parent, but don't be afraid to help your daughters learn to be tough. Encourage them to take risks and allow them to make mistakes. This is how they will grow, get better, and find out who they are. Do you wish for you kids to accomplish more than you did, to be more confident and successful than you are, and to do more than you have ever done? If so, push them, support them, and be tough on them. Expect more from them, then encourage, love, and support them at every turn.

Stop protecting your kids. Expect as much from your daughters as you do from your sons. Parents have a tendency to protect girls more. Girls have a tendency to be more emotional and dramatic, and they fight with words. I suggest you engage their emotional and dramatic tendencies because those are powerful skills, but teach them to be thoughtful with their words. Words may be used as weapons and may hurt others. To communicate with young women, you must be present and truly listen.

Live your own life and let your kids live theirs. As a coach, I've seen far too many parents trying to live their lives and achieve their dreams through their children. This is destructive to everyone, especially your child. Many times, the parents become the problem. One of the most successful high school coaches I have known retired from coaching because of the out-of-control and destructive behavior of some of his player's parents. His life was threatened over the phone by one of his player's fathers. After this incident, he retired at the end of the season and went home to his family and newborn baby.

In another incident, a colleague looked out his window and saw that a mean-spirited person had placed a "for sale" sign in his yard, encouraging the coach to move and to leave town. Really? There will be times that are great and triumphant, and other times that are challenging, unfair, and difficult, but allow your kids to navigate issues themselves. Kids need to learn to fail and to take risks in order to build their own resilience. If we don't start at a young age we are setting them up to fail as adults.

Young women should be taught how to have direct conversations with their coaches and teachers. Your daughter needs to learn how to stand up for herself and to learn to exude power and confidence. She should become accustomed to asking for what she wants at a young age so she is prepared to do so as an adult.

In Chapter 3, a young woman I met learned how to have a hard conversation with an adult at the age of 17. Soon after that, I had a similar experience in New York. Four sets of mothers and daughters approached me. They were pursuing dance and their coach had humiliated one of them just a few days before. The young sixth-grader now lacked confidence and showed low self-esteem. Teach them to have this hard conversation with their coach at a young age. Support them and back them up.

Moms and dads approach me and ask for advice about their daughters every day. It is a hot topic and many parents are searching for answers and advice. It is a significant responsibility to prepare your kids for what's down the road and out in the real world. Don't fight their battles, but do support and encourage them every step of the way. They will survive and, eventually, thrive. This is exactly what they need to reach their dreams and to be ON POINT.

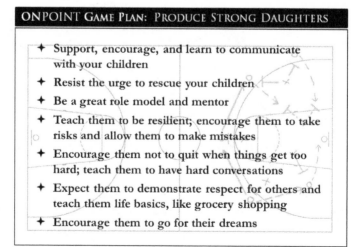

ONPOINT GAME PLAN: PRODUCE STRONG DAUGHTERS

+ Support, encourage, and learn to communicate with your children
+ Resist the urge to rescue your children
+ Be a great role model and mentor
+ Teach them to be resilient; encourage them to take risks and allow them to make mistakes
+ Encourage them not to quit when things get too hard; teach them to have hard conversations
+ Expect them to demonstrate respect for others and teach them life basics, like grocery shopping
+ Encourage them to go for their dreams

ADVICE TO MY YOUNGER SELF

"Often the best gift you can give yourself is time alone,
some time to ask your questions and listen quietly for answers."
—Katrina Mayer—

For the title of this chapter, you could very well use the cliché: If I Knew Then What I Know Now. Unfortunately, life is unidirectional. You don't get to go backward, only forward. We all learn from our past successes and failures, but it's always onward and upward. No backtracking, no do-overs.

I wish I could bend the space-time continuum, writing myself letters from the future. I'd open my email in the morning and a message from my future self would await me. *Good morning,* it would say, *Here's what you need to know today . . . have a great day!*

MAKE IT BETTER

My first piece of advice to my younger self would be to leave things better than you found them. I achieved this when I was let go from my head coaching position at the University of Minnesota in 2014. After a successful career, I left the program in great shape; the cupboard was stocked with talent, our student-athletes graduated and achieved a 3.0 grade point average every year, and our program boasted a league-record 88 Academic All-Big Ten honorees over my tenure. And, I left on a high note as the winningest coach in program history. The program was sustainable, it would flourish without me, it had the right players on board, and it had a solid foundation of talent and values. This platform would continue the program's success, hopefully, for a very long time.

I would also say to my younger self, as you go through life focus on being in the right seat on the bus and surround yourself with the right people. And, when you leave, you'll know you did well if there's sustainability and continued success. Poor leaders leave an unsound, unstable foundation that crumbles immediately upon their departure.

To my younger self, I would clarify my top five values that I live by personally and professionally. I would say to implement these values as early in your life as you can and never waiver:

1. Integrity

2. Honesty

3. Hard work

4. Teamwork

5. Family

Good things happen to good people and I believe that things happen for a reason. When you leave a situation, don't expect to ride off gloriously into the sunset. In my former world, that's rare. After the immediate shock passed, I viewed my transition from the University of Minnesota as a blessing and a gift, not as a firing or as if I was being let go. And as I noted in Chapter 12, giant doors opened for me . . . doors, plural. The same can happen to you when transitions occur in your life, if you embrace them. Don't feel sorry for yourself during transitions, but embrace them and know that there is something better out there, if you go get it. No one will give anything; you have to earn everything you get.

Dr. Seuss said, *Oh, the places you will go.* His book by the same title is one of my favorites, and was a gift I would give each one of my players as they graduated from college. I would write a personal note on the inside of the cover for each player about the opportunities they would have in all of the places they would go.

When transitions occur, I guarantee if you choose to engage your purpose and passion, and choose to thrive, your realms of influence will expand from small to large and opportunities will follow. When facing difficult challenges in life, I would tell my younger self to be resilient and determined. Never quit. Don't shy away from the public eye, but embrace it. Face it head on and it will make you stronger than ever.

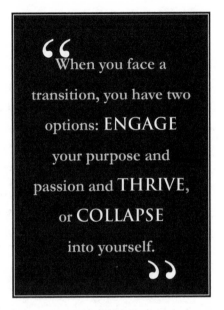

"When you face a transition, you have two options: ENGAGE your purpose and passion and THRIVE, or COLLAPSE into yourself."

I made an interesting observation during my transition from basketball coach to business coach and consultant. When I was down following my dismissal, many of those around me quickly disappeared. Those who were with me at the top disengaged and exited my life; it was disappointing, but also refreshing. There are points in our lives when we need to weed certain people out and to weave new ones in to lift us up and make us better. Our lives change and so do the people with whom we associate.

With my feet planted firmly at sea level, I sought out new people. And new, amazing people entered my life. These people changed my life and, in some cases, saved my life. These angels helped me navigate and find my way through a very difficult transition, and to approach a different world and profession. This support network remains with me and, to supple-

"Invest in PEOPLE who invest in YOU."

ment them, I have surrounded myself with some of the best friends and business partners I could ever ask for. There is always a point in your life where a transition WILL happen, so rely on your true supporters and look for new, terrific colleagues around every corner.

PEOPLE MATTER

I would encourage my younger self to get a mentor. We may think we know it all and are ready to take on the world ourselves. We may believe we have all the answers. Listen to and learn from your mentor. Pay attention and learn as much as you can from people who have more experience, who have richer knowledge, and who have been there and done that. You haven't, so learn from people who care about your success. Find a mentor who will take you under their wing and guide, support, and encourage you to take risks. A mentor will provide you with direction and accountability, which you will need.

I would tell my younger self that it's never about me. It's about the people I surround myself with—it's literally about other people. We can get caught up in that lead position, as the top dog moving up the ladder, quickly. When we get to the top, we don't realize that there's still much to do. It's overwhelming, it's hard, and there are many challenges—we can't do it all, by ourselves.

In order to be successful, you must have a strong bench. A strong bench, filled with key supporters and talented teammates, is crucial to reach your goals and to achieve success. I would tell my younger self to surround yourself with a staff and a bench that compliment your strengths. Don't surround yourself with people you want to like you, a bunch of "yes" people, people who are just like you and think like you, but people who will challenge, push, and offset your weaknesses with their strengths.

I would tell my younger self that the toughest part of a job is hiring. I don't know if you feel the same way, but it's incredibly difficult to find competent, hard-working people with the right attitudes and values. Recruiting, hiring, and maintaining the right fit is one of most difficult parts of the job. Don't hire fast, hire slow—this was some of the best advice I received from a mentor when I began to hire my own staff. Take your time and hire slow. Hire people who share the values that align with your program, team, and organization.

Learn early to delegate and to elevate others so they can also experience success and gain confidence. I would tell my younger self that good leaders are great delegators. This starts with hiring capable and talented people and then allowing them to do their jobs. Stay out of the weeds as a leader, please. When you rely on others, architecting an environment in which they can succeed, you give yourself more time for strategic leadership and build sustainable skills in your team members. And, they will thank you for trusting them and for adding to their capabilities.

I would tell my younger self to learn to be a better listener and to ask more questions. Learn this as early in your career as you can. If you think you're a good listener, listen more. Do more listening than talking. Listen, learn, and allow others to share their opinions and ideas. Many leaders have a difficult time doing this because they are not secure or patient. They will interrupt, shoot an idea down, get defensive, and disregard an idea from their team. They will quickly rush to a resolution, relying more on their own perspective and experience, and fail to build ownership and buy-in.

I would not surround myself with contrarians, but I would find people who are not afraid to share ideas and to challenge me to get better. I have always thrived when surrounding myself with people who challenge me with creativity and innovation in a healthy way. Such an environment makes us all better and gives us added leverage to reach our goals. Today, I continue to surround myself with challenging, creative people.

I would tell my younger self to always treat people with respect. Respect defines the type of leader you are. To be respected as a leader, respect the people around you, all the time. Value everyone no matter what his or her role is in your organization or on your team. Respect is a low-cost, high-value gift that secure leaders easily share with those around them.

It is so much better to give than to receive. I would have never thought this way as my younger self. I received so many gifts—of knowledge, of opportunity, of support—that I am now a passionate philanthropist and enjoy giving back and paying it forward. The feeling when I give back is like no other. Helping people fulfill their wildest dreams is one of the ultimate pleasures in my life.

PASSION AND BELIEF

I would also tell my younger self to nurture my passion for the game of basketball, because it will lead to more than just the game. Working my way up to the head coaching chair, I didn't realize the wonderful game of basketball would lead me to bigger, more meaningful opportunities and to heights I never imagined. There's more to the game than winning and losing. It's about the process and enjoying the journey. If you focus on just the wins and losses, it will consume you and eventually eat you alive.

Finally, I would tell my younger self that I believe in you, so believe in yourself. There will be moments of self-doubt and, certainly, times when others doubt you. Don't let these times paralyze you or divert you from your path forward. Keep your chin up, know that you can and will succeed, and welcome the opportunity to learn about yourself. We all have barriers and challenges we must face; you will overcome them if you believe in and trust in yourself.

> What comes easy **WON'T LAST,** and what lasts won't **COME EASY.**

Yes, my email box would have filled up with letters from the future. Obviously, I would tell my younger self a lot, but I would not change one thing about my process of growing up and becoming an ON POINT leader. I have no regrets and I wouldn't trade the scars and the cheers for anything. Life is all about failures, successes, and life lessons; it's a terrific gift to grow and to find out who you are by taking risks and by experiencing this on your own.

ONPOINT GAME PLAN: ADVISE YOUR YOUNGER SELF

+ Define the top values you will live your personal and professional lives by daily
+ Focus on your strengths, continue to work on areas of improvement, and surround yourself with those who complement you
+ Embrace transitions in your life
+ Weed people out and weave new people in that lift you up and make you better
+ Be resilient and determined and believe in yourself
+ Remember that it's not about you; focus on others and treat them with respect
+ Give back and pay if forward, always and often

PART FIVE

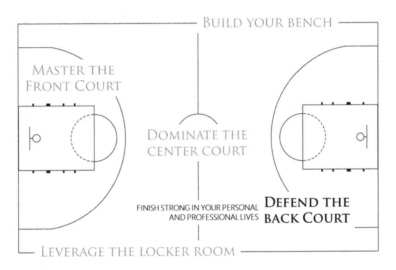

BUILD YOUR BENCH

MASTER THE
FRONT COURT

DOMINATE THE
CENTER COURT

FINISH STRONG IN YOUR PERSONAL
AND PROFESSIONAL LIVES

DEFEND THE
BACK COURT

LEVERAGE THE LOCKER ROOM

LIVING WITH CLASS

"Class has nothing to do with money. Class never runs scared.
It is self-discipline and self-knowledge. It's the surefootedness
that comes with having proved you can meet life."
–Ann Landers–

Are you a leader who can't get your team on the same page, moving in the same direction to accomplish a common goal? Leadership requires the capability to translate an inspiring vision into reality. A great leader needs to start with, and believe in, a compelling vision. Being able to share and communicate the vision, define roles and responsibilities, then inspire action are critical to achieve a desired outcome.

CLUELESS AND CLASSLESS

I was watching one of my top recruits play one night in one of my frequent visits to this high school and their games. It was a powerhouse for girls' basketball programs in the state and they were recognized nationally. As I sat alone watching the game, one of the player's parents was seated a number of rows behind me in the stands. As the game progressed, the player's parents spun out of control and began yelling at their daughter. The volume kept getting louder and frequency increased, and their comments were getting brutal. I was extremely embarrassed for them. No class. Parents are supposed to support and encourage their kids, not criticize and berate them in front of a crowd.

It wasn't even halftime yet and I was planning on moving my seat. I couldn't stand to hear any more nonsense. The horrific words these parents shouted were making me absolutely crazy. My embarrassment for them grew as their poor behavior continued; they had no idea how foolish they looked and sounded, but they were about to find out.

In the middle of the second quarter, the daughter of the classless parents turned the ball over right in front of our seats. The play did not stop—and neither did the parents' mouths. Then, something shocking happened right in front of my eyes: the player who turned the ball over, as she was running back on defense, turned to her parents and flipped them both off. I was stunned but inside I wanted to give her a standing ovation. She'd had enough. Can you imagine what she was going through, listening to the hurtful words from her own parents? Enough was enough. I won't say it was right for her to flip off her parents, but she broke. Where was the role modeling? Well, the modeling was happening all right, but it was with no class.

I will never forget that night in the gym—both what I heard and the reaction. After the player's message was sent, their voices were silent for the remainder of the game. A few times I turned around to see if they were still there because it was so quiet. They were still sitting there. They got the message and whether through embarrassment or rationality, they decided to shut their mouths. Class is knowing what to say, when to say it, and when to stop. It stopped, but the damage was done.

What's disappointing is that I could write so many more examples just like this. We see and read about parents and fans coming out of the stands after coaches, officials, and players. Parents slide out onto the ice, run onto the field, or jump onto the court. I've heard and seen it all. When they don't like their kid's roles, disapprove of a lack of playing time, or see that other players are the coaches' favorites, they even get coaches fired—especially at middle school and high school levels.

What is really happening? Their status and value as a parent is tied up in and played out through their kids. Their deep investment in their child's success, and (often unreasonable) hope for scholarships and stardom, manifest in a desperate need for perfection and result in frustration at any misstep. It's really sickening. Go stand on the sidelines of a youth game and watch 11- to 13-year-olds play. Go to a boys' or girls' junior varsity or varsity high school game—hockey, football, soccer, lacrosse, basketball, baseball, wrestling—the sport doesn't matter. You will notice that some parents do not sit or stand with other parents. Why? If you're a parent, look around; is anyone sitting near you? Are you the parent who has chosen to sit away from the others who are losing their minds, or did they move away from you? Do you see parents watching their kids play a sport they love? Do they still love playing?

Hopefully, others look at you and say, *There's a class act.* You support, encourage, embrace, cheer, and know what to say, when to say it, and when to stop.

IN SEARCH OF CLASS

Tragically, we've lost a sense of class in our communities and in the workplace. Class is exercised in your community, professional, and personal environments. Class is you, the person, and how you treat others, your ability to project empathy, and your commitment to always do the right thing. To be successful, you must have an essence of class within and an aura of class around you. As you think about class, consider how you present yourself, how you treat people, how you project maturity, and how you address and respect others.

The demonstration of class—or a lack of it—is a major issue for leaders in business. Apply my parent-player story to your workplace environment and culture. Are you that person who is "yelling from the stands" at your people and teams? Do your team members want to "flip you the bird" (or even worse)? Is your boss the one doing the yelling?

A great leader is always a class act. I coach clients on their emotional intelligence and help them learn to become self-aware and to control their emotions. Most often, leaders usually fall to one extreme or another on the emotional continuum. Some leaders focused so intently on being liked that they fail to communicate expectations clearly and can't create accountability. As a leader your focus is not to be liked, but to be respected. On the other end of the spectrum, there are leaders who are brutal, blunt, harsh, and disrespectful. They may hide behind a motto of "telling it like it is." They are ineffective leaders and they won't earn respect from their people and teams. Great leaders know what to say and how to say it to engender respect and trust.

I was a head coach for 12 seasons on the Big Ten's sidelines. I experienced the biggest and most heated pressure situations, but I never, ever was called for a technical foul in a game. In fact, in all of my years as a head coach, I never had one technical called on me due to my behavior. Officials knew me as a professional on the sidelines; they knew I treated people fairly, respected others, and rarely got upset to the extent of earning a technical. Sometimes I wonder if I could have won a couple more games if I picked up a couple of technical fouls, using them to influence the officials or fire up my team—but that wasn't my style.

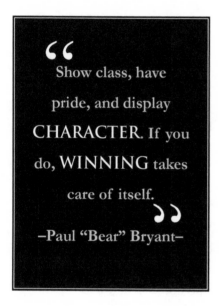

> Show class, have pride, and display **CHARACTER. If you do, WINNING** takes care of itself.
>
> –Paul "Bear" Bryant–

I learned as much from my players as they learned from me. Now I'm learning as much from my clients as they learn from me. Do you have this mindset? Stop and think of all the things you've learned from the people around you. I didn't realize this until the last few years I was coaching college athletics. Step back and be present. Learn as much if not more from the people you are leading. Be a class act.

CLASS PRODUCES LUCK

You've probably heard people say, we need some luck to go our way. I don't believe in luck; I believe in hard work. I believe we create own luck and opportunities. In my experience, a tremendous work ethic results in good things happening to good people. That's a class act.

Class is a key ingredient to luck. Being a class act is critical in a leadership position, especially if it's one that's in the public eye. You are being watched ALL the time. There is no hiding, you are always on, and when you close your office door at night, you're still on. Keep this phrase in mind: if you see me doing it, then it's OK for you to do. This goes for good behaviors, like working hard, or bad, such as cutting corners. People who do the right things, and work the right way with class, will find themselves presented with great opportunities.

As a coach, I would always say to my players, what you do off the floor is what you will do on the floor. There is a correlation between displaying class and demonstrating integrity in our lives through consistency, discipline, organization, and work ethic. I was called many things as a coach, but the most common (and most welcome) label used by parents, officials, donors, stakeholders, and people I didn't know who watched from afar was "a class act." I pride myself in how I treat and respect all people, on and off the court. I expect the same from my clients as leaders—to lead with class at work and in their lives.

While there are many benefits of being a class act, one key benefit is drawing others to you who are class acts. My network was broad, but now it has expanded nationally in the business world. In 2014, I was honored with a global award in being a connector. As an influencer who is connected and connects others, the award recognized my commitment to go far beyond the walls of higher education and athletics, to think globally in connecting others across industries. Why did my life evolve this way and, eventually, lead me to receive this honor? I am driven, I am a doer, I show up, I care about other people's success, and I do it with class. My passion and expertise is connecting with people. You can do this, too.

In the Fall of 2014, I traveled to Thailand to coach and to consult with an organization. It was a great opportunity to get global experience and to work with a cross-cultural team. I leveraged this experience to the fullest in business and athletics. While I was there working, I found an English charter school and volunteered my time coaching basketball to American and Thai girls of all ages. I spent four afternoons at the school teaching basketball and consulting with the school administration, and spoke to an audience of teachers about leadership. I learned as much from them as they did from me.

We control our own destiny and I have controlled mine most of my life. I'm a believer in setting goals and having high expectations for myself and others. I set "Big Bucket Goals" each year and I hold myself accountable to these personal and professional goals. I carry them with me in my notebook, everywhere I go; you can do the same. I have learned to surround myself with people who live this way also.

My commitment to live my life with class resulted in one of the paramount relationships of my life, and the one that bolstered my success most significantly: finding the perfect life partner. Living with class creates luck, and I am the lucky one.

People with class are winners. They uphold principles of integrity: doing things the right way, treating people with respect, and acting with honesty. These people persevere and are always rewarded at some point in their lives. They are ON POINT and know what being a class act is all about.

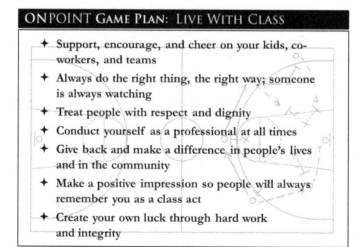

ON POINT GAME PLAN: LIVE WITH CLASS

+ Support, encourage, and cheer on your kids, co-workers, and teams
+ Always do the right thing, the right way; someone is always watching
+ Treat people with respect and dignity
+ Conduct yourself as a professional at all times
+ Give back and make a difference in people's lives and in the community
+ Make a positive impression so people will always remember you as a class act
+ Create your own luck through hard work and integrity

WINNING IN LIFE

"Winning is great, sure, but if you are really going to do something in life, the secret is learning how to lose. Nobody goes undefeated all the time. If you can pick up after a crushing defeat, and go on to win again, you are going to be a champion someday."
—Wilma Rudolph—

In the competitive worlds of athletics and business, the psyche of winners has been well-documented and extensively studied. My experience characterizes the winner's psyche in terms of a proven ability to put forth consistent effort, to dedicate countless hours to preparation and to the establishment of routines, and to persevere regardless of the challenges. The winner continues to dedicate concerted effort until they accomplish their goal and their own expectations in their life and their work.

Intention is critical to the winner's psyche. The concept of winning has become central in our society—in sports, in business, in politics. Everything we do seems to revolve around this dynamic. We all know the age-old refrain: *Winners never quit and quitters never win.*

There's a direct correlation between effort and reward. The victory never tasted sweeter than when you have prepared for hours, days, months, and years for it. With victory, everything builds exponentially; your confidence, morale, and desire increase the more you win and the more you fear losing it all. Once you taste victory, you want more.

JUST WIN, BABY

Before you create a game plan to win, you need to define what winning means to you. We all identify and define winning differently in our lives. It depends on the intersection of why, where, who, and how. Why do we need to win: for what purpose? Where are we: at work, at home, on the field, on the stage? Who are we with: teammates, coworkers, clients, family members, or friends? How will we win: as a team or as an individual?

We may define winning based on our self-expectations and needs. Look in the mirror and ask yourself, *Am I winning in my life?* If the answer is *yes*, what does this mean? Where have you won and how are you winning? If the answer is *no*, then why not? What are you missing and how are you defining winning in your life?

As you consider what winning means to you, use the following framework to evaluate your approach to winning. If you haven't addressed these items, take action.

1. *Define Goals.* Set specific goals in your life, at least each year. Everyone needs a road map. If you don't know where the finish line is (your vision and goals), you're not going to get anywhere.

2. *Own Your Actions.* Stop blaming others. Stop making excuses. Winners are self-aware and admit to their mistakes and accept their vices; understand the responsibilities that come with your choices and decisions. Find solutions, work harder, and surround yourself with people who will make you better.

3. *Develop a Winning Habit.* Vince Lombardi said it best: *Winning is a habit.* Sounds simple, but how do you develop this habit? Challenge yourself and get out of your comfort zone at home and work. Keep it up until you start to feel more comfortable.

4. *Don't Fear Failure.* There are enough inspirational quotes and stories in this book to remind you that winners and leaders who are ON POINT

are the ones that fail, pick up the pieces, and move on. Failure means learning life lessons. Lean on this, let it motivate you. It motivates me!

5. *Value Life-long Learning.* Ask questions, be curious, talk to people inside and outside your industry, read articles and books, and stretch yourself to learn new things. We all can continue to get better by broadening and deepening our knowledge and connections.

6. *Take Risks.* Yes, it is safe to stay in the harbor, away from the churning seas—but you'll never explore new horizons or visit far-away lands. Seize each day, pursue the maximum return on your heartbeats, and don't miss an opportunity. You may not get a second chance when an opportunity arises.

7. *Focus.* What is it? Focus creates seriousness and seriousness creates action. Focus is one of the most powerful tools in athletics and business psychology. Laser focus on the right things. You will erode your confidence focusing on the wrong things.

8. *Be Committed.* The primary difference I see day-to-day for those that feel they are winning is their commitment and drive in life. Winners know what they want and they are doers. They go get it. They have a vision of what winning in their life is and they take action to get there.

9. *Work Harder and Smarter.* You must be willing to work harder than most. I bet you feel like you already do. If your competition is doing 100 push-ups every day, you have to do 200. Working smarter is also crucial; be more efficient and more effective. More effort in a smarter direction usually results in success in work and life.

BEYOND THE SCOREBOARD

Winning is more than the score on the scoreboard at the end of the game or match. Winning in life means so much more to me than winning games. I have won a lot of games (305 to be exact, in 16 years as a head coach) and I was consumed with winning daily. Winning and the result on the scoreboard determined if I kept my job or not. However, at some point in all of our lives, winning won't be enough. It's in all of our best interests to define what winning and success mean to each one of us.

It took me awhile to wrap my head around what success and winning meant to me. Now that I am older and wiser, and have experienced the black-and-white of winning or losing my entire career as an athlete and coach, I realize I only knew one way to think and to act. It was the scoreboard that determined everything for me. The big video boards and jumbo-trons determined my success as an athlete and as a coach. It made sense, but I still searched for a bigger underlying meaning and definition of winning in my life.

I was very fortunate that I grew up with a solid and loving family, with both parents and three sisters. My parents have been married for more than 56 years; observing their unconditional love and having a supportive family my whole life was foundational to my development. My parents watched every basketball game I played from fifth grade to my senior year in college. They also supported and watched me coach for 27 years. They were able to watch me grow as a coach and person, to live my passion, to see my mistakes, and to experience my successes and biggest games on the biggest stages. In total, they watched me play and coach a game I loved until I was 48 years old and it was a big part of their lives. Sharing this part of my life with my family, sisters, brothers-in-law, nieces, and nephews was winning in my life.

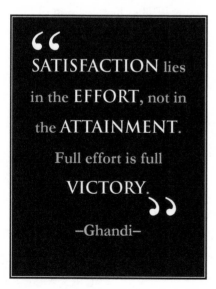

Winning in my life also is having a life partner who makes me better and challenges me every day. The unconditional love, the tremendous career support through the heartaches, and staying home alone while I traveled the world for my job were sacrifices many would never make. Even when I was home, I wasn't home. My mind often was somewhere else, preoccupied, watching film until early hours in the morning or talking on the phone with recruits until the late hours of the night. We would come home early from our vacations because something happened at home with one of my players. Every college coach needs to have such a special person in their corner. Only other head coaches and their spouses know how deeply important this is.

Winning in life also is having the best of friends any one could ever ask for. My best friends were always there for us, through the good and bad. They would come to the majority of my games at Minnesota's Williams Arena and sit and cheer me on to victory. They knew what kind of lives we lived and what was at stake, sitting in the stands behind my bench in the same seats for 12 years. They survived snowstorms, expensive parking ramp costs, losing seasons, traffic jams, and blowout victories. Winning in life is having friends like this. No matter where you are, they are always there for you.

Winning in life is being crazily, madly, and insanely connected with your passion and purpose in life. It is when you are surrounded with people who make you better, who love you for who you are and not who you've been, and who want success for you as much if not more than you do. I'm lucky to have these people in my life.

Are you making a difference, creating an impact in people's lives, leaving the place better than when you found it, and paying it forward to help others? If so, someone paved the way for you, someone helped you get to where you are today, someone encouraged you and pushed you to be uncomfortable—winning in life is giving back and paying it forward.

Winning in life is to accomplish something great and to leave a mark and your legacy. Look at your family, friends, kids, job, community, players or coworkers, parents, or your pets—are you winning in your life? You may be an accountant, a lawyer, a doctor, in the military, a schoolteacher, a coach, a professional athlete, a mother, or a stay-home dad. How do you define winning in your life?

Are you winning? Does winning mean that you have a big house, make lots of money, and have a big title? Does winning mean you have raised a wonderful family; that you have great kids who are off to college and you're in a healthy relationship? Or, does it mean you have strong faith, you travel the world, you're retired, and you're doing exactly what you want and with the people you want in your life? Define what winning means to you, then get ON POINT and go after it.

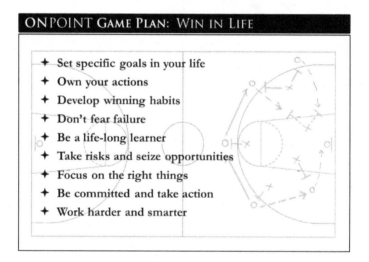

ON POINT GAME PLAN: WIN IN LIFE

+ Set specific goals in your life
+ Own your actions
+ Develop winning habits
+ Don't fear failure
+ Be a life-long learner
+ Take risks and seize opportunities
+ Focus on the right things
+ Be committed and take action
+ Work harder and smarter

FINDING
YOUR HOME

*"There's a whole world out there and you have to begin
by letting people see who you really are."
—Dorothy from the Wizard of Oz—*

There are many reasons why the Wizard of Oz is one of my all-time favorite movies. I have two Yorkshire terriers, Bentley and Stella, so I can relate to Dorothy and Toto trying to find their way back home. As we age, movies like this develop a different meaning; often, our advancing wisdom and perspective identify messages about people and relationships. When is the last time you watched The Wizard of Oz? I often think about what Glinda the Good Witch said to Dorothy: *Home is a place we all must find. It's not just a place where we eat or sleep. Home is knowing. Knowing your mind. Knowing your heart. Knowing your courage. If we know ourselves, we're always home, anywhere.*

Have you ever noticed how dangerous familiarity is? The more frequently we observe our surroundings, even the unique and beautiful, the less we actually see them. We often take for granted the opportunities and variety the whole world has to offer. Of course you've heard the adage, the only constant is change. I want you to consider the four walls around you right now. Are you stuck in a silo? Do you look at everything through one lens?

It is common to think and to feel this way if you don't expand outside your area of expertise or your industry and you don't get a different view from the outside.

Different ears and eyes, thought processes, perspectives, and voices are extremely helpful to break out of our silos. Here are some important actions you can take right now: identify your gifts, position for opportunity, broaden your horizons, and be creative and take flight.

IDENTIFY YOUR GIFTS

Your gifts represent specific, meaningful skills you have that are well beyond mediocrity. You can't be an expert at everything, but you are certainly an expert at something. You're only at your best when you are following your passion, when you have a clear vision, and when you're taking the proper steps to achieve success. Do you have your gifts identified correctly?

Consider when you were a child; what did you love to do? There is much to be discovered even as an adult. For me, I loved to play basketball. I wanted to be the best. So I practiced and played during all of my free time when I wasn't helping out on the farm (and, of course, when my homework was completed). I converted this passion into a career playing and coaching basketball until 2014.

Two weeks after I departed from the University of Minnesota, I stepped back and took stock of my gifts and passions. My focus and life was changing trajectory, so I drew out a visual road map that displayed many lily pads on a piece of paper. Some of the lily pads focused on starting a business, which was daunting and something I'd never done before. Once I sorted out the ideas I'd captured, I focused on the goals that were important to me; it started as a "wish list" and then became an action plan to accomplish. The tasks became my focus, reinforced my passion for coaching, and gave me milestones; I was determined to reach them all. In my first year as an entrepreneur, I accomplished nine out of the 10 lily pads and started two businesses and two non-profits.

These images of the lily pads helped identify my path forward and kept me focused on my purpose and intentions. A big triple-paned door had opened into the next chapter of my life. Home is knowing your vision, where your heart is, and where you belong. When you know your heart, you will feel empowered and energized and you will fill in the blanks.

Your path to your dreams will be your own. Make it one that no one has ever walked. I've always been motivated by not following the herd—the most successful people run the opposite direction! Nothing motivated me more than being told I couldn't do something. Those words always carried significant impact for me, motivating me beyond the point of determination. If someone tells me today that I can't do something, I will attack it with vigor and nothing will stop me from succeeding. It's a part of my DNA.

Know your heart, identify your gifts, and begin doing what you love. If the primary objective is to put one foot in front of the other, moving toward something that gives you passion will help you get out of the gate and maintain momentum when the going gets tough. An object in motion tends to stay in motion. Once you start moving, do it at only one speed—GO—and don't let barriers block your path. Every possession in a game, every day, and in everything you do, remain focused on knowing your heart and having courage. Start with your network, ask for feedback, and know that it's good to ask for help. Be brave and take a chance.

POSITION FOR OPPORTUNITY

Set aside time for self-reflection. If you are in a career that does not make you happy, what are you doing to change?

As I write this book, the U.S. has a $16-trillion economy. There is ample opportunity in this economy to find or to create meaningful work that aligns with your passion. It is a huge pie and you can find your piece. You've simply got to put yourself into a position to take advantage of the opportunity our country (and the whole world beyond) affords.

Opportunities for growth abound for business owners, entrepreneurs, and independent contractors. Tremendous growth is occurring in these sectors. By their nature, most corporations do not favor individual stars. The consistent focus of large organizations is to replicate structured tasks and consistent outcomes. However, many organizations are starting to move in the direction of creating self-directed, high-performing teams and implementing leadership development strategies. While many are lagging behind, almost all companies now know what direction they need to go in terms of talent acquisition, development, and retention. There are opportunities for you to learn and to grow in these organizations. If your organization isn't on track, find one that is.

Money doesn't make you happy—freedom does. Consider how many people in your life, right now, could make a major decision (good or bad) that would change your life overnight. Such a person may be a boss, someone who buys your company, a colleague, an employee, or a team member. One way to minimize the risk a life-altering decision is to plan ahead: diversify yourself by broadening your skills, expanding the entities and people with whom you associate. Spread your eggs among various baskets. Avoid having only one person, customer, client, or boss who could make or break you.

> "
> There are two kinds of people in the world: energy GIVERS and energy TAKERS.
> Who are you going to surround yourself with?
> What type will you be?
> "

Here's another straightforward way to guard against such a situation. Sun Tzu's *Art of War* recommends that you keep your friends close and your enemies closer. I really didn't know what this meant until I experienced and survived many difficult times professionally. There are so many applications of this tactic, but until you live through it yourself you will never fully understand. There are always people around you who are insecure and jealous and want to see you fail.

I have been asked many times why people are like this; there are people who are jealous of success and they take joy in watching (or helping) successful people fail. It's sad but so true. I'm tempted to name a few . . . but I won't. So, get to know identified or potentially hidden "enemies" and you may be able to limit their damaging influence—or at least be prepared when the lightning bolt may strike.

BROADEN YOUR HORIZONS

There's a whole world out there, one that is spectacular and interesting. Get out of your four walls at work and escape the silos of your business and industry. There is so much more to see and learn. I was in my own silo for 27 years coaching college athletics. I had no idea what was beyond those walls, outside the arenas, gyms, and locker rooms that were my home; it's all I ever did and all I thought I knew how to do. When I left those four walls, my eyes opened and I was amazed at how much I was missing and by how many opportunities to learn and to grow had surfaced. It was exciting that there were and are vast opportunities to transfer my coaching passion and skillset to business and corporate America, for teams big and small.

What was I afraid of? Nothing. On the other side of those doors awaited opportunity, healthy change, and new challenges. It was energizing! My 27 years of coaching basketball prepared me for what was next and any challenge I may face.

There was nothing I couldn't do. I had learned empathy, velocity, authenticity, and values; I could coach and develop people to their full potential and I knew how to navigate very difficult situations as a leader with grace.

I inventoried my gifts and strengths, I was in a position to take advantage of opportunities, and I wasn't afraid of what was ahead.

" The world is but a **CANVAS** to our **IMAGINATION.** "

–Henry David Thoreau–

TAKE FLIGHT

It was clear coaching was in my blood and, as a true coach, working with people and teams is my calling—just not in basketball. Now I interact with titans of the business world and community leaders who need a rudder. Many leaders want a coach to collaborate with: to be a thought partner, to provide support, and to help them navigate their pressure-filled, stressful, ever-changing world. They want assistance and reinforcement to manage the complexities of people and teams and to align them to perform cohesively and competently when the stakes are high.

I'm that rudder and I coach these leaders by providing the direction they need to achieve success. I'm the compass in the wilderness that points the way forward and the road map that holds them accountable to develop their ON POINT leadership skills to reach the next level. I'd been doing this my entire life, just in a different venue. I just needed to think creatively to find new, different arenas in which to exercise my skills. What I had the passion to do for 27 years prepared me for what I was meant to do today.

Home is a place we all must find. I found mine; I just took a much different path than most. I found my home: motivating and developing others to be successful is my value proposition and what makes me unique as a coach.

As Dorothy traveled to and from the Land of Oz, she discovered she was a great leader who helped others realize the talents and substance inside of themselves. She did not know how she was impacting the Tin Man, the Cowardly Lion, and the Scarecrow—she just followed her heart and courageously pushed forward. In this day and age, effective leaders lead by creating the conditions and providing the resources and opportunities to help the people around them and their teams find what's inside each of them. ON POINT leaders bring out the best in people.

Home is knowing. Knowing your mind, knowing your heart, and knowing your courage. What's inside of you? Where is your home? You'll have to find out yourself. But what I do know and I have experienced myself, is that a whole world—an amazing, opportunity-rich world—welcomes us out there.

Glinda was right: *Home is a place we all must find.* If we know ourselves, we're always home, anywhere. Know yourself and let people see who you really are, authentically. I found my home and I thank all the people along my journey for preparing me for what I was really meant to do: to coach others to be ON POINT and to achieve the next level.

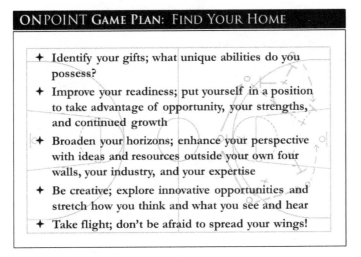

ON POINT GAME PLAN: FIND YOUR HOME

+ Identify your gifts; what unique abilities do you possess?
+ Improve your readiness; put yourself in a position to take advantage of opportunity, your strengths, and continued growth
+ Broaden your horizons; enhance your perspective with ideas and resources outside your own four walls, your industry, and your expertise
+ Be creative; explore innovative opportunities and stretch how you think and what you see and hear
+ Take flight; don't be afraid to spread your wings!

A TRUE COACH
IS RARE

"A coach is someone who tells you what you don't want to hear,
who has you see what you don't want to see,
so you can be who you always knew you could be."
—Tom Landry—

I had an interesting conversation with a colleague about what constitutes a "real" coach. So many people will claim the title of "coach" as athletic coaches, executive coaches, and business coaches, but are they really and truly effective coaches?

Many executive and business coaches have never applied their recommended solutions in a real work environment or in practical situations as a leader, or have ever led a team. Many have studied and researched it, read about it, and received countless certifications (even PhDs), but few have ever felt the blazing heat in these situations themselves or sat in the lead chair.

Athletics and the military offer excellent laboratories in which to develop and to identify true leaders. My good friend, a U.S. Navy veteran, will smile when he reads this because I have so much respect for him. We've worked together in business and we are very much alike despite the different paths we've traveled. We "get" leadership, teamwork, working together for a common goal, and the understanding that if one fails, we all fail. There's a lot of talk about the theories of leadership, but many of those coaches have not been exposed to an arena in which to develop true leaders or to serve as leaders themselves.

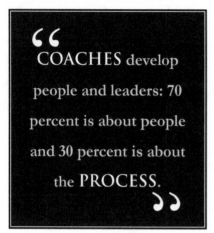

> " COACHES develop people and leaders: 70 percent is about people and 30 percent is about the PROCESS. "

There are many leadership books but no reliable manual that enables one to become what is a rare, hard-to-find product: a *True Coach*. How would you rate yourself as a coach? Do you want to be coached by someone who has lived it or someone who has just read about it? If you believe you are a coach, or you have the privilege of working with a coach, rate him or her using the following six characteristics and behaviors of a True Coach.

1. *Listening.* Are you an active listener? Listening to your players, kids, staff, and clients is vital to being a great coach and leader. This is a sign of security and confidence. Stop talking and listen. When you listen, do it with the intent to truly hear—not to wait until the person stops talking so you can say what's on your mind next. Try and keep you mind clear and open to the message you are hearing and to the way the person is delivering it. The eyes, tone of voice, and posture often tell the story better than words.

2. *Demonstrating accountability.* First, do you hold yourself accountable? Modeling is one of the most important things we do as leaders. Eyes are always watching you. Are you holding your kids, players, and staff accountable? You will get exactly what you expect—of yourself and others.

3. *Developing trust and loyalty.* The quickness in which a real coach can develop trust and loyalty is remarkable. How do you develop trust and loyalty? Real coaches can do this at lightning speed. The ability to develop trust this rapidly builds a great player/client/employee-coach relationship. Always demonstrate honesty and integrity in your actions. Then,

if you care about your players, employees, and clients and you are there for them, on and off the court, in and out of the office, you will develop instant trust. Treat trust reverently; it evaporates as quickly as it forms if you have mistreat it.

4. *Delivering feedback.* Real coaches have the ability to deliver constructive feedback, positive and negative, to people of all different types and styles. They have an innate sense of people and of the ways in which to inspire and to motivate to help players, employees, and clients reach their full potential. Feedback is a gift, especially when it is delivered immediately, strategically, positively, and constructively. Once you've developed trust, feedback displays that you care and you want that person to succeed.

5. *Communicating with flexibility and versatility.* There are many different types of people, situations, and communication styles. Real coaches know how to communicate effectively under pressure, stress, and chaos. How do you manage your emotions under pressure and stress? It's easy and anyone can do it when things are going well. Real coaches and leaders can handle and manage themselves with consistency in the heat of the moment. You must be emotionally self-aware, know your hot buttons and pet peeves, and be able to manage them during times of stress and chaos. I learned to stay even keel at all times, to give myself 24 hours to deal with intense or sensitive issues, and to remember that I was ON POINT. My handling of every single situation was under a microscope so I always modeled my best behavior. I would repeat one of my favorite mantras to myself: *Things are not always as good as they seem and things are not always as bad as they seem.*

6. *Ensuring self-development.* True coaches and leaders are life-long learners. They stay relevant, curious, and creative and are always striving to achieve their personal best. Learn from the team members you lead and from other leaders. One of the best ways to learn is to meet with people. Learn what they do, how they do it, and why. Get out of your industry and explore diverse work environments and business cultures.

It took many years of preparation and practice, success and failure, and joy and pain to learn the keys to being a real and true coach. My players were my best teachers; your best teachers are the people you lead. I did not realize how much I learned from them until I could step back, look at the big picture, and understand that leading involved much more than winning and losing. It was about being a genuine coach, a mentor, a role model, and a learner.

The pressure of college athletics offered temporary wins and losses, but knowing that my team members would benefit from and remember the impact I had on them for the rest of their lives represented a lasting and significant legacy. We all have the responsibility and opportunity to create a legacy with people and teams we lead every day. While I coach my clients to be ON POINT, I learn as much from them as they do from me.

Each of the six characteristics and behaviors of a true coach resonated with me as I became seasoned and worked to enable my players and team to perform at their best. I had to win games—that was the bottom line—but I learned that winning was more than what appeared on the scoreboard. The keys to true coaching were as crucial then, with my job on the line every season, as they are now with my clients and the teams I coach in the business world. Now, it's their jobs on the line—they have to win and that's the bottom line.

True and real coaches are exceptionally rare. They are leaders who demonstrate class and grace no matter what the situation. How do you rate your leaders and yourself in the six characteristics and behaviors of a true coach? Now more than ever before, your children, players, clients, teams, and team members NEED you to be that coach. They need you to be ON POINT and to believe in, and deliver on, this mantra: *I am a True Coach!*

ONPOINT GAME PLAN: BE A TRUE COACH

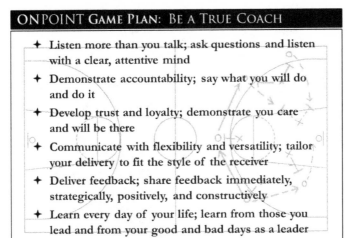

+ Listen more than you talk; ask questions and listen with a clear, attentive mind

+ Demonstrate accountability; say what you will do and do it

+ Develop trust and loyalty; demonstrate you care and will be there

+ Communicate with flexibility and versatility; tailor your delivery to fit the style of the receiver

+ Deliver feedback; share feedback immediately, strategically, positively, and constructively

+ Learn every day of your life; learn from those you lead and from your good and bad days as a leader

ENJOY THE JOURNEY

"It is good to have an end to journey toward;
but it is the journey that matters, in the end."
—Ernest Hemingway—

I'm guilty. I'm guilty of having too much focus and of not taking time to enjoy the journey. This chapter is as much for me as it is for you.

When the buzzer sounded and the game was over, I will never forget what it felt like to win the biggest game of my career. Beating Duke to advance to the Final Four was a process and journey I enjoyed the entire way. My staff hugged me, we were jumping up and down, and my players ran to the sideline and jumped into my arms. I have never seen a group of young women so happy with tears rolling down their faces. I am also a very emotional person and I had tears streaming down my cheeks in my assistants' arms, on my players' shoulders, in my athletic director's embrace, and as I looked up in the stands to my parents and Lynn.

I t was all so surreal. Then, all of the sudden, I felt one of my players grab me from behind and the team picked me up off my feet and carried me off the floor to the tunnel. They grabbed the Gatorade cooler and dumped it over my head with ease. That was the best bath I had ever experienced—a Gatorade bath. My hair, my suit, and shoes were soaked and all I could do was put my fist up in the air and say . . . *We did it!* There were more hugs and tears because we accomplished something special for the state of Minnesota and our Minnesota family.

The ladders came out and all the players ran to the locker room to get their own individual scissors that we'd handed out the night before the game. They were going to use the item that symbolized what winning this game would mean to them. As I climbed the ladder to cut a piece of the net, I remember every step I took until I was able to grab the net. As I cut down the last piece of the net, I looked down at my team, the fans, and my family and held up the net because this was the biggest day of my life. We all were so happy; we enjoyed every moment because we knew the grind we'd endured for a long eight months to reach this monumental day. We were on our way to New Orleans for the program's first appearance in the Final Four.

We all need to stop, pause, reflect, and enjoy each and every moment in our lives. Be present, aware, and appreciative. I made this mistake many times, losing myself in the process and focusing only on the wins. Through my surreal journey, enlightened by highlights of Big Ten and NCAA Tournament wins, the perfect storms, and organizational challenges, I opened my eyes to the process, the journey, and its treasures.

I am achieving my goals and chasing my dreams in life, in full-on pursuit mode. It's exhilarating and I find joy in it every day while enjoying the journey. I used to chain myself to a series of tasks in Spartan-like self-denial. I tried to enjoy my journey and the process, but only with a constant reminder from my very dear mentor, my former athletic director and friend. He reminded me frequently to *stay the course.*

He was always there for me, especially during the difficult times—after the most heartbreaking losses and when everyone else turned away. He was always the one who reminded me to enjoy the journey and believed that everything happens for a reason. His words of encouragement came in a text, email, or a phone call when I needed them the most. Before and after every game for 10 years, I received a text that said, *Good luck, Great win,* or *Let's get ready for the next one.* My last two years coaching, even when he was no longer my boss, I still received those texts and he remained one of my biggest fans and supporters.

Who wouldn't want to work for a boss like that? His personal approach is a lost art in any industry; someone that busy, at that level, took the time to demonstrate empathy and compassion to his head coaches. This doesn't happen at many places. Where are these leaders? Are leaders ingrained with these qualities today or did they break the mold? Everyone wants to be around an ON POINT leader who inspires, picks you up, and reminds you to enjoy the journey during the wins and the losses. If you're not enjoying the journey in your business, life, and relationships, it's time. If so, continue reminding yourself and others because this will have a significant impact on your life—it did for mine.

I had the pleasure of spending a week with a very successful retired emergency room doctor from Arizona while I was working on my Executive Coaching certification in Santa Barbara, California. For whatever reason, we really hit it off and we continue to support one another in our second careers. I thought I had a stressful job coaching college athletics;

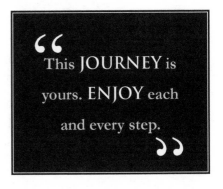

> " This JOURNEY is yours. ENJOY each and every step. "

he was an emergency room doctor where the stress, pressure, and people's lives depended on him to be an ON POINT leader at all times.

We went for a run together one sunny day before class started and I asked him, *Have you enjoyed your journey?* He looked over at me and didn't speak for a minute, and then he said, *Pam, no one has ever asked me that before.* I said, *We all need to be reminded of this as we go through life . . . it's easy to get caught up in the daily stresses, pressures, emergencies, and reckless pace, and forget to enjoy the journey.* I will never forget the special exchange we had because it was the first time he'd ever heard or considered such a thing.

Challenging others and myself to enjoy the journey, shines a light on several life lessons:

1. *The world enjoys playing with us.* The ins and outs of our lives are filled with humor. Avoid taking yourself, and your life, too seriously. Trust me; an overly serious approach causes unfathomable stress, undue pressure, and unrealistic expectations. Weave humor into your life rhythm and you and the people around you will be happier and full of gratitude.

2. *People matter.* It's pretty simple: people matter. I have said it throughout this book. Surround yourself with good people—those who give you energy, make you better, and challenge you to be the best. Empowering, inspiring, and making a difference in the lives of others is rewarding. Looking into someone's eyes changes the conversation. Lead. Inspire. Listen. They will follow.

3. *Take care of you.* Your physical, mental, emotional well-being are critical. If you don't take care of yourself, how do you expect to take care of others? The ability to manage anxiety, stress, and the mental aspect of what we do is an important life skill and most don't know where to begin. Exercising and sustaining a healthy lifestyle have been keys to my energy level, emotional well-being, and ability to positively affect others. If you don't take care of yourself, you will dampen your enthusiasm, darken your outlook on life and, at times, you will get physically ill. Taking care of "number one" is critical in enjoying your journey.

4. *Keep your eye on the prize.* I've always been a visionary and strategic leader. My dreams and vision drive me every day. People close to me have always described me in one word: *determined.* I accepted the job at the University of Minnesota because I believed we'd have a chance to win a national championship. We were close, reaching the Final Four and being just two games away from winning it all.

5. *Move on to the next play.* Learn to forget, have a short memory, and move on quickly from your mistakes. We all have a tendency to hang on to a mistake or a failure. Sports teach many life lessons; the ability to move on in our lives, relationships, and businesses after making a mistake is important for growth. Here's what I tell my clients when they make a

mistake or they feel bad about a decision or a situation: *Apologize for your part, then move on to the next play and don't dwell on the moment.* I would tell my players something similar: *One mistake leads to two, two leads to three, and then you'll be sitting on the bench next to me.*

6. *Celebrate small successes.* During my basketball coaching career, I did not do a very good job celebrating small successes and enjoying the wins. I hated to lose more than I enjoyed winning. Over time, I learned that winning is extremely hard and that enjoying small successes is part of the journey. The head coach's chair was lonely and putting out fires all day seemed to be the norm. If you're building a program or business, or recovering from failure, celebrate the small successes and throw confetti and pop champagne for the big wins. It's the only way to continue taking positive steps forward and to keep your energy level high.

7. *Be present.* Be in the moment and slow down to enjoy your surroundings: the sights, smells, sounds, smiles, and the people. You never know if you'll ever experience those treasured moments again. I may never cut the nets down again or feel a sticky-sweet Gatorade shower. Many times it's a once-in-a-lifetime experience, so pay attention and soak it in.

The Final Four, Sweet 16s, the upsets, and the sell-out crowds in Williams Arena were pinnacle moments and terrific accomplishments, certainly. When I look back, proud and completely satisfied, I know I could have savored those and other moments even more. I remember the process, but did I enjoy it, relish it, and appreciate all the people who were involved as much as I could?

Be ON POINT in the moment. If you take the opportunity to savor the moment, the world will respond to you differently. It did to me. That may sound cliché; however, when you have joy in your life, so do the people around you, and the world smiles back.

ONPOINT GAME PLAN: ENJOY THE JOURNEY

+ Take time to reflect on where you are and what you have achieved; celebrate small successes on the way
+ Be present and appreciate your surroundings
+ Ask yourself and others: *Are you enjoying your journey?*
+ Add fun and humor into your life; don't be too serious
+ Focus on the people around you
+ Take care of your well-being
+ Keep your eye on the prize; go after your dreams
+ Move on to the next play and leave mistakes behind

ABOUT THE
AUTHOR

As the winningest coach in the University of Minnesota women's basketball history and now top-performing, International Coach Federation (ICF) executive coach, keynote speaker, and author, Pam Borton's life purpose is dedicated to taking individuals, teams, and organizations to the next level.

Pam stands apart with 27 years of high-level, NCAA Division I coaching experience, including 12 years as head coach at the University of Minnesota. She led her teams to a Final Four, three straight Sweet 16s, and seven NCAA Tournament appearances as a head coach. Having successfully navigated the pressure and expectations of a highly visible position in an ultra-competitive environment, Pam now brings that unique background to her C-suite leaders, senior-level leaders, and teams in the business world.

A multiple award-winning recipient, Pam has been honored with the Top 10 Global Women of Leadership Pillar Award, Ann Bancroft Dream Maker Award, (Real) Power 50 Award, *Twin Cities Business* Marvelous Mentor Award, and New England National Coach of the Year. She was a two-time Naismith National Coach of the Year nominee.

To further expand Pam's life purpose and passion, she co-founded Team-WomenMN in 2011, a Minneapolis-based non-profit dedicated to empowering women to reach their full potential. In 2014, Pam also founded the Empower

Leadership Academy for girls in grades 5 to 12, a non-profit whose mission is to develop leadership skills among girls and young women. As a result, Pam was honored with the creation of the Pam Borton Endowment at the University of Minnesota in the College of Education and Human Development—the only endowment of its kind in the world.

In addition to founding Borton Partners in 2014, an executive coaching firm, she delivers dynamic keynote presentations nationally. She is co-founder and co-owner of Women On Point: Next Level Leadership, a venture to deliver elite leadership development summits for women.

ACKNOWLEDGMENTS

Our lives are a journey and I have been so blessed my entire life with so many people—those who have come and gone like gentle breezes or hurricane-force winds, those who have stayed for decades like stout oak trees, and the new people I meet every day who bloom vibrantly in bright colors.

There are so many people to thank because I surely did not get here myself. Through growing up on the blacktop, playing college basketball, having the honor to coach at four great institutions and universities, and now opening up a new world after leaving athletics, the people I have met and those I have now in my life give me the strength, wisdom, knowledge, support, and inspiration to be my best. I'm the luckiest person alive to have had my family and friends by my side throughout the journey.

If you want to make an impact of significant contribution, then you have to do things you either don't enjoy sometimes or that are not your strengths. Writing this book was a big undertaking for me, and others around me, because I do not consider myself a writer. It took me longer to write it than it should have; most people who know me know that I can't sit still for long and I always need another project and to be on the move. I began working on this book thinking that I could draw on my lifetime of practical and real experience coaching athletics; then, as I started coaching and consulting in business, I slowed my writing pace so I could integrate and weave athletics and business together because they share common leadership challenges. In the experience of that realization, like when I hiked the Inca Trail in Machu Picchu in the summer of 2015, I discovered in my life that I hadn't reached the summit in my life or career at all, just the top of the first rise. From this new vantage point only visible at the peak of a mountain like this—gazing through my blood, sweat, and tears—I set my sights on the real mountain and began the new climb. All that I had experienced for 27 years in coaching college athletics prepared me for what was next: the new chapter in my life.

I literally went through this experience many times, each time thinking I had finally reached the summit, each time convinced that the book was finally "done," and each time humbled by the realization that I had only achieved yet another critical level of insight and experience. I traipsed over several false summits only to find more heights to reach the mountain's peak. Finally, I reached a vista that allowed me to complete the book, yet I know as a life-long learner that there will be more climbing ahead for me to enjoy. I know in my heart that there is so much more and I look forward to it.

The greatest and most inspiring mountain-climbing achievements are not the individual accomplishments and awards, but they are the narrative stories of the extraordinary power of a unified, talented, prepared, high-performing team that stays loyal and committed to one another and to their shared vision and values until the very end. Most people and teams that set out to accomplish big goals together or to climb the highest mountains never reach the summit; only the privileged few make it to the next level. For one reason or another, most people and teams, when pushed to the limits or out of their comfort zone by extreme conditions of adversity and the strains of working under fire, drop out and quit, choosing to turn back because the work just got too hard. The story of my climb of Machu Picchu, my achievement of the NCAA Final Four pinnacle, and now my objective to be the best executive coach, is no different. Were it not for the determination and unwavering resilience, commitment, dedication, support, and encouragement of a committed and loving team that helped me with this project, the book would have failed to be completed. They pushed me, shared their talents and efforts, and held me accountable every step of the way.

I have mentioned Lynn many times throughout this book with utter awe for the support and encouragement she's provided me on this journey. Life for a coach's spouse is insane and I'm not sure I could have switched roles. She's been my biggest supporter, confidant, voice of reason, and life partner in every sense of the word. She left me a note on the kitchen counter every morning for 12 straight years while I was coaching at the University of Minnesota. Her unconditional love is the wind beneath my wings.

I can't thank my family enough. Where would I be without you? My parents started attending my games when I was in the fifth grade and they stuck it out until I coached my last game at 48 years old. For 30 years, they sat in the bleachers and behind the bench and they were the only voices I could hear from the stands. I know they will always be "behind my bench" and their voices of encouragement will echo forever in my heart and soul. To my three sisters and my nieces, nephews, brothers-in-law, grandparents, aunts, uncles, and cousins, I thank you for your love and for the gift of all the memories and experiences growing up that shaped my life. To my in-laws and the rest of the family, thank you for enjoying this journey with us. Thanksgiving trips with the team will always be deeply embedded in our memories. I love you all.

I want to thank my truest of friends. The truest of friends are there for you no matter what you are experiencing, good or bad. While in Minnesota, I had a small core of very close friends who were always there for me through the ups and the downs. They had my back all the time and they spent long nights in the stands, supporting me more than watching the game. They attended many of my games during my last two seasons. We laughed together, we cried in each other's arms, we vacationed together—they are my extended family. They are the people we plan to spend the rest of our lives with—you know who you are.

I'm very fortunate to have good friends from all over the country in the athletic and business coaching profession. We never lose track of each other and we stay in contact no matter where we are. Our friendships run deep.

A special thank you goes to Aimee Cohen, who pushed me throughout the entire process of writing this book. There were many days when I said I didn't want to do it, that it didn't matter if I finished it or not, but as my coach, project manager, business partner, and best friend, you pulled and pushed me across the finish line. We all need people in our lives who force us out of our comfort zone and who push us to do things we don't want to do. You always had the big picture in mind for me, not for yourself, and this gift is one of the greatest I've ever received.

Kevin Burkett believed in me from the first time we met at People's Organic. Two strangers brought together for a reason, Kevin and I met weekly for six months and he was instrumental in helping me write this book. Our weekly meetings, sharing our personal and intimate stories, and his views as a very successful business owner, entrepreneur, and extremist, gave me a whole new perspective on life. The framework you gave me to start adding my stories and my words to the book was invaluable. I would have never written this book without you and your friendship.

Adam Cohen had a vision for the final manuscript, beginning with coining the title ON POINT. Then, when he probably thought he'd done his duty, he was a lifesaver down the stretch, helping me creatively and technically with content editing and restructuring, manuscript formatting, cover layout, and graphics design. You came through down the home stretch and took ON POINT over the finish line. The relationship I have built with your family has been a gift and a blessing at this stage of my life, and one I will endeavor to keep forever.

It is with deep gratitude that I express my appreciation to the following for their support and talents, and for believing in me:

- ❖ All of my mentors inside and outside of the industry. To my former athletic directors, bosses, and colleagues, thanks for giving me the opportunities of a lifetime and for believing in me. I learned more from you than you will ever know.

- ❖ All of my former players. To literally hundreds of former players whom I loved like my own daughters, and I still do, thank you for making an impact on my life and for adding more value and purpose to life than you can imagine. I learned as much from you as you did from me. I am proud of you all.

❖ All of my former assistant coaches. I value and thank you for all of your hard work and dedication, and for caring as much as I did. You are all doing great things and changing lives.

❖ All of my former support staff, managers, and scout teams. You always mattered and were always the most valuable people in the organization.

❖ All of my former and current clients, and the organizations, individuals, and teams in business I coach today. I am honored to have your trust and I appreciate the opportunity to learn from you.

❖ All the fans and supporters who followed my teams throughout my coaching career. The memories of your support wash over me like a wave, even in my infrequent quiet times. It was a great ride.

❖ Kristie Smith at Yellow Finch Communications, a very talented editor on the manuscript editing team; you played your role like a champion.

❖ Kristen Moeller at Morgan James, who believed in me and my story and supported me as one of their authors. Your team took the final manuscript and raised ON POINT to the next level, published the book, and distributed it worldwide.

❖ Sandy Poirier Smith at Smith Publicity, whose passion jumps through the phone line like no other; and Kristi Hughes, thank you for your day-to-day grind and expertise in public relations across the country.

❖ Amy Sinclair, for being a great friend, serving as executive director of my TeamWomenMN non-profit; you are passionate, caring, and so giving of yourself to others. You're making my vision become a reality.

❖ Jennifer Hartigan, serving as executive director for the Empower Leadership Academy for Girls, my second non-profit; you see, share, and believe in the same vision of developing leadership skills and confidence in our girls, our next generation of leaders.

❖ Finally, and so significantly, all of my former coaches in the sports of basketball, softball, cross country, and track in high school and college. Every one of my coaches, at one point or another, made the biggest impact on my life. You inspired me to perform at my best and, now, to reach for and to achieve the next level in my life.

We made it! Individually, these three words look small and non-descript. Together, they comprise a mighty statement. I used these words many times throughout my life and career. I said these words when I reached the top of Machu Picchu, and I will continue to use these words throughout the rest of my life because that is the only option.

WE MADE IT!

ARE YOU ON POINT?

EXECUTIVE COACHING AND CONSULTING

Borton Partners brings an International Coach Federation (ICF) certification, passion, and a proven track record of success to C-suite executives, emerging leaders, athletic coaches, teams, and organizations. We provide support, structure, and accountability to sharpen the leadership skills of top producers and to take them to the Next Level. We offer a highly customized approach to meet the needs, and to exceed the goals, of our clients. If you're looking for a true coach to develop a strategic game plan and take you, your team, or your organization to the Next Level, then let's get started.

Whether it's to resolve an urgent situation or to address longer-term issues, allow Borton Partners to bring decades of coaching experience and expertise to make a positive impact. The biggest difference between amateurs and professionals . . . is coaching. Often times, the greater the success, the greater the isolation. You don't need to go it alone any longer. With a trusted coach and thought partner by your side, you can take your leadership skills to the next level.

KEYNOTE SPEAKING

Pam Borton motivates and compels action through practical and inspiring keynote speeches and breakout presentations—always customized and targeted to meet the unique needs of the teams, groups, and individuals.

She has addressed and provided team-building for groups of all sizes and in all segments, including government, non-profit, higher education, athletics, and the private sector. Invite her to address your group, professional association, company, division, or team.

TEAM-BUILDING

If your team or group is ready to get ON POINT, a customized session is your ticket to success. From half-and single-day seminars to multi-day workshops, let Pam and her team guide you to the success you desire and deserve.

For more information, visit www.pambortonpartners.com.

A free eBook edition is available with the purchase of this book.

To claim your free eBook edition:

1. Download the Shelfie app.
2. Write your name in uppser case in the box.
3. Use the Shelfie app to submit a photo.
4. Download your eBook to any device.

Shelfie

A **free** eBook edition is available
with the purchase of this print book.

CLEARLY PRINT YOUR NAME ABOVE IN UPPER CASE

Instructions to claim your free eBook edition:
1. Download the Shelfie app for Android or iOS
2. Write your name in **UPPER CASE** above
3. Use the Shelfie app to submit a photo
4. Download your eBook to any device

Print & Digital Together Forever.

Snap a photo

Free eBook

Read anywhere

The Morgan James
Speakers Group

Morgan James makes all of our titles available
through the Library for All Charity Organization.

www.LibraryForAll.org

CPSIA information can be obtained
at www.ICGtesting.com
Printed in the USA
BVHW070738230119
538421BV00004B/4/P

9 781683 500209